THE STORY
OF THE CIVIL WAR

THE STORY
OF THE CIVIL WAR

by
COLONEL RED REEDER

Illustrated by FREDERICK CHAPMAN

DUELL, SLOAN AND PEARCE
New York

Library of Congress Catalog Card No.: 57-5561

Fifth printing September 1960

MANUFACTURED IN THE UNITED STATES OF AMERICA

VAN REES PRESS   •   NEW YORK

ACKNOWLEDGMENTS

I appreciate receiving from Colonel Vincent J. Esposito, professor and head of the Department of Military Art and Engineering, United States Military Academy, West Point, New York, permission to use material from *Civil War Atlas*, which he edited. Most of the maps in this book are based on maps in *Civil War Atlas*.

I am indebted to the following for making unpublished letters available: Colonel William J. Morton, the librarian at West Point (letters of Captain James Crozer, 26th Iowa, and a letter pertaining to Brigadier William R. Terrill, U.S. Volunteers, killed in action at Perryville, Kentucky); Mrs. Mabel Alice Davis, of Fredom, New Hampshire (two letters of a front-line infantry soldier, Private Samuel Moulton, 9th New Hampshire Regiment).

My wife, Dort Darrah Reeder, gave care and attention to the numerous stages of the manuscript. I owe her a debt of gratitude for this, for her counseling, and for her encouragement.

RED REEDER

Dedicated

to

WILLIAM LEE MILLS, JR.
*Major, 12th Infantry Regiment
United States Army*

A fearless battlefield leader of World War II

CONTENTS

THE STORY
OF THE CIVIL WAR

Chapter 1

THE FORT ON THE SAND BAR

FIRE flashed from a cannon. An iron ball screamed as it arched across the harbor and smashed into the island fort. The next cannon ball skipped on the water and exploded in the rocks at the water's edge, its fragments spraying the walls.

For a moment the spirits of the sixty-four Northern soldiers inside Fort Sumter rose. The first shots had battered only a few bricks. The men let out a cheer for the flag fluttering above them, the Stars and Stripes.

To the South Carolinian soldiers working at the shore batteries around Charleston Harbor that flag was the symbol of the hated North. The Southerners regarded Fort Sumter as an enemy stronghold in their territory and the men inside, wearing the blue uniform of the Union Army, their deadly enemies. The South Carolinians were determined to capture both the fort and its small garrison.

Men, women, and children poured out of Charleston to watch the bombardment. They crowded every vantage point. At the shore batteries the gray-clad Confederate soldiers worked to better the aim of the cannons. The harbor rang with the thunder of guns, as shots smashed into the fort from three directions.

3

Inside the fort the men were under great stress. The wreath of smoke from the black powder made it hard to return the enemy's fire. The explosion of the cannon balls and the pounding of solid shot against the walls were nerve-shattering.

Major Anderson, the United States Army officer in command of the fort, was worried. He knew he was up against an expert artilleryman, for he had instructed General Pierre Beauregard when the Southerner was a cadet at West Point. Major Anderson knew he was outnumbered, sixty-four against ten thousand, and there was little food in the fort's commissary except salt pork.

Three months before the battle, Anderson's soldiers had seen the United States government vessel, *The Star of the West*, loaded with supplies, approach their fort. The Confederate shore batteries opened fire, but Anderson would not let his men shoot to aid the steamer because he wished to avoid war. The men in the fort watched helplessly as the ship turned her nose to sea and her paddle wheels drove her out of range of the guns.

Hotheads in Charleston were delighted that their cannons were at last pounding the hated Yankees in their island fort. A few wiser ones wondered if the South had enough men and materials to challenge the North. The pompous General Beauregard assured the people of the city that the Yankees would not fight hard. He gave the impression that as long as he was in command the Southern cause would succeed.

After repeated bombardment of the Union fort, Beauregard sent two aides to demand that Major Anderson haul down the Stars and Stripes and surrender. The wooden barracks were on fire, and the powder magazine was in danger, but Anderson refused to surrender. However, he unintentionally gave valuable information to the enemy when he said to the two aides, "Gentlemen, if you do not batter the fort to pieces we shall be starved out in a few days."

So of course General Beauregard kept up the cannonade. At the end of the second day's fight, Major Anderson had to surrender the fort. He asked for permission to salute the Stars and Stripes before he hauled down the flag. He wanted to march out with banners flying, his band playing "Yankee Doodle." Beauregard gladly granted the major's wishes.

In the salute to the flag, one of Anderson's guns burst, killing a private soldier and wounding several others. This sad accident added to Anderson's misery over the loss of the fort.

General Beauregard allowed Anderson and his men to board a steamer and sail for New York. Both sides were very courteous. The Union and Confederate armies had not yet begun to battle to the death or to throw their prisoners in horrible prison camps. This was April, 1861, a critical date in American history.

Beauregard quickly became the hero of the Southland, and he liked the part. He was an odd-looking fellow, dark-skinned, with large black eyes and drooping lids. Often when he spoke, or wrote, his manner was vain. Songs and poetry were written about him. He was the man of the hour at a time when the South was busy raising armies. Many Southerners believed that his regular army background and his success against Anderson at Fort Sumter made "Old Bory" the ideal choice for over-all commander of the Southern armies.

Oddly enough, Major Anderson was received in the North as a hero, too. His action at Sumter, while it was not a last-ditch stand, was what the Secretary of War in Washington, fearful of touching off a war, had ordered. Anderson was hailed in New York City with wild enthusiasm. He was quickly promoted to brigadier general. Everyone knew that he and his men had braved the Southern cannons, and although he had surrendered, Anderson became a symbol to his countrymen.

The man in the White House was Abraham Lincoln. He was determined to preserve the Union. The day after the flag was hauled down at Fort Sumter, President Lincoln called for 75,000 volunteers, each to serve ninety days. Many Yankees thought this unnecessary, for they did not expect the war to be a hard one or a long one.

A wave of flaming enthusiasm for battle swept both the North and the South. Both sides began arming as fast as possible for one of the greatest wars known to man, a war of more than two thousand battles.

Chapter 2

A TOTAL MISUNDERSTANDING

WHAT caused the Civil War?

What caused a war so terrible that the deaths on the Northern side alone amounted to almost 400,000?

The Southern armies were so shaken by defeat in this war that no one knows accurately how many Confederates were killed or wounded. It is reasonable to suppose, if the Northern side lost 400,000, that the South lost an even greater number.

Historians do not agree on the basic cause of the Civil War. Every student of this period has his own answer.

Feeling ran high in both North and South in 1861. If you asked a young man living in Mississippi in March of that year about the situation facing the country, he might have replied like this:

"I am ready to fight for my country—the South. Think of Senator John C. Calhoun. He was one of the smartest men we ever had in this part of the country. He was Secretary of War and Vice-President of the United States.

"Old Calhoun outargued the best the Yankees could put up, Daniel Webster. Calhoun proved that a state has the right to set aside any gov'ment law which does not help the state. It would be downright stupid for us to stay in the Union the way they pass laws to hurt us. And, besides, they don't back up their laws.

"Take slavery, for instance. The Fugitive Slave Law says all runaway slaves must be returned. How many have been returned to their owners? I'll tell you. Very few!

"And most of the Yankees say that slavery is wrong. Well, if it's wrong, why doesn't the Bible say so? We've had slavery in this country since the time of the Colonies. The Yankees brought in the first slaves and they have made plenty of money selling them South. The Northerners are not only trying to wreck slavery, but us.

"The Yankees organized an underground railroad to help our slaves escape to free states and to Canada. About 70,000 slaves have been helped to get away from us down here. It's not a real railroad. That's the name they have for the people who help the Negroes escape.

"Up in Massachusetts they got a wild man named William Lloyd Garrison. He burned a copy of the Constitution and said that, if necessary to free the slaves, the Union must be dissolved. Why didn't they arrest him?

"That book, 'Uncle Tom's Cabin,' by Harriet Beecher Stowe, is stirrin' up trouble. If we had an overseer on our place as mean as Simon Legree, the overseer in that book, why, we would run him off. We take *care* of our slaves.

"About that President they just elected, Abraham Lincoln. We don't trust him. Lincoln actually said he's going to keep the Union together at *all costs!* You know what that means.

"Well, if they want to fight, let 'em come on. It's a known fact that one Southerner can lick six Yankees. Our side is right and we'll fight for what we believe. The Yankees don't understand us at all."

But if you asked a young man living in New York about the state of affairs he might have answered like this:

"The best thing that has happened lately is that we now have a *man* in the White House. Abe Lincoln. He's not a blueblood, he's a man of the people. He was born in a log cabin in Hardin County, Kentucky. He grew up in Indiana and made his way as a lawyer in Illinois. He's smart, strong, and honest. He knows what's best for this country.

"Abe Lincoln says, 'A house divided against itself cannot stand.' He means, of course, about the Union having both free and slave states. He's absolutely right.

"The Southern states are leaving the Union. Can you have a country where a state can pull out whenever it feels like it? Abe Lincoln won't put up with that, for it will wreck the country. There'll be a war first, and it's not far off.

"We've tried compromises and agreements, but nothing seems to work.

"Do you think it's all right for one human being to be able to own another just because his skin is a different color? Why, it's *morally* wrong!

"I read that best seller, 'Uncle Tom's Cabin.' They have three paper mills running night and day to furnish paper and ten printing presses printing it. That book gives you a true picture of slavery. How'd you feel if you had to be sold down the river from your mother?

"Do you think the South has enough men to win the war that's coming up? I don't. We have almost nineteen million people. The South has only nine million. The border states—Kentucky, Maryland, and Missouri—seem divided right now, but wait till the shooting starts!

"We in the North have many industries that will help in a war. What has the South got? They have very few factories. They can help themselves by selling their cotton, but suppose Old Abe and the United States Navy blockade their ports. Then where will they be? We have forty-two men-o'-war and we'll build more. They have none. I expect they'll build some, but we have a head start on 'em.

"Our side is right. The Southerners don't understand us at all."

The entire nation was disturbed by hotheads on both sides who talked wildly, without reason. The Abolitionists demanded the slaves be freed AT ONCE! They exaggerated the plight of the slave, picturing him as tortured. Abolitionist posters announced, "We cannot be too hasty in carrying out our designs." They were not worried about a civil war or wrecking the Union. So wild and so laced with hate were their plans, the very word "Abolitionist" came to mean "hateful" to the entire country.

The country was also inflamed by the "fire-eaters," rabble-rousing orators. Charles Sumner, of Massachusetts, abused Southern statesmen in Congress. Robert Rhett, of South Carolina, shouted from lecture platforms that for the South to exist the Union must be dissolved immediately. Robert Turnbull, of the same state, told Southerners that they must stay with the South on every question. "It's a case of sink or swim," he said. William Yancey, skillful lawyer from Georgia, argued long and loudly that the South must secede from the Union. Southern orators gave out the idea that sooner or later the federal government would use soldiers to impose the will of the North. The Abolitionists and the "fire-eaters" helped bring on the war.

Chapter 3

WAR DRUMS BEGIN TO BEAT

A TALL man wearing a black suit and a stovepipe hat walked slowly up the long steps of the State, War, and Navy Building in Washington. When he reached the top, he touched a finger to his hat to return the salute of the policeman on duty at the door.

"Hot day for May, isn't it, Mister President?" said the policeman.

Abraham Lincoln's Adam's apple moved slowly up and down. The wrinkles around his gray eyes softened.

"I've learned to expect 'most any kind of weather here in Washington."

Down Pennsylvania Avenue, in a cloud of dust, came a company of marching soldiers. They were singing. The soldiers' uniforms made them look as if they were going to a fair rather than preparing for war. They wore red trousers, short white leggings, blue jackets with brass buttons. Strapped to their backs were black leather knapsacks. Each man shouldered a long rifle with a swordlike bayonet fixed at the muzzle.

"Zouaves from New York, sir," said the policeman. "Volunteer infantry. I wish you could see 'em drill, Mister President.

They can do every fancy step in the book. 'Specially good at the quickstep."

The Zouaves were singing a parody of the new song "John Brown's Body":

> *We'll hang Jeff Davis to a sour apple tree*
> *We'll hang Jeff Davis to a sour apple tree*
> *We'll hang Jeff Davis to a sour apple tree*
> *As we go marching on.*

The officer at the head of the column recognized the President and saluted with a flourish of his sword. The soldiers stopped singing and cheered Lincoln as they marched by.

The guard spoke. "Only trouble is, catching the Confederate President won't be as easy as it says in that song."

Inside the big building Abe Lincoln listened as General Winfield Scott, the head of the United States Army, went over war plans. Scott was a battle leader and looked it. The only trouble was that he was seventy-five years old.

The huge general rested a hand on the gold-handled sword lying on his desk. That sword had been presented to him by his native state, Virginia, in honor of his victories in the War of 1812. He wanted to stand up at the map while he talked to his commander in chief, but he was so heavy and in such poor health that it was difficult. General Scott blew his nose. It sounded like thunder in the distance.

"We have a big job ahead, Mister President," said the old general. "The best thing is not to make a move till we have well-trained soldiers, sir. When we have 'em, let's send an army down the Mississippi River Valley to slice the Confederacy in two. This will cut off their supplies from the Great Plains of Texas, and we'll take the seaport of New Orleans. In the meantime our ships can stop Confederate ships from going in and out of every harbor on the Southern coast. Then our armies can fight the Confederate armies in Virginia, or wherever they may be. We have a gigantic task."

Lincoln stroked his lean chin. *Would the country have the patience to wait until we have a well-trained army?* Lincoln respected the famous soldier. But others in the capital did not. They said that he was too old.

Scott leaned heavily on his desk to support his tremendous weight. He pointed a finger at the map. "The worst thing, sir, would be a direct attack against the Confederate capital in Richmond."

Scott was right. To do that, with the Confederate armies blocking the way, would be like compressing a heavy spring.

"If only we had a larger regular army, Mister President," said the old general mournfully, "we could put down this rebellion at once. Many lives would be saved, because the Confederates are straining to get ready just as we are."

But there were fewer than thirteen thousand men in the regular army and they were scattered over the entire country. Many soldiers would have to stay at frontier posts and fight Indians.

"We are just not ready, sir," continued Scott, "but we have to keep our patience."

An aide came in and saluted. "Excuse me, General, but there are a number of West Point cadets outside. I mean, young officers who recently graduated from West Point. They want to see you, sir."

The wrinkles disappeared from Scott's brow. His hard, turned-down mouth smiled, for he liked West Point cadets and he liked the Military Academy. He saw clearly the value of both, although he was not a West Point officer himself.

"Fine!" said Scott. "What do they want? How many of 'em are there?"

"Forty-one, sir. They've come to tell you that they don't want the vacation they've earned at West Point. They want to be sent to units which will soon be in the fighting."

The new lieutenants were smart in their blue uniforms and forage caps. Each wore a black shiny pistol belt and holster. In the front row was young Judson Kilpatrick, a New Jersey boy, who would soon be the first regular officer to be wounded. Three men in this class would win the Medal of Honor.

Both Lincoln and Scott spoke warmly as they welcomed the young officers into the service of the United States. It was a pleasure for Lincoln to see low-ranking officers who wanted only a chance to fight. Every day many citizens came to the White House to see him, asking for commissions as generals and for other important positions. Some who were after high rank brought their congressmen along.

Many sad good-bys were said in the United States Army. Men who had served together under the trying conditions of the Mexican War and who had fought side by side against the fierce Indian tribes prepared to give everything they had for either the Stars and Stripes or the Confederate Stars and Bars.

Families that were divided in allegiance were torn by bitterness. William R. Terrill, an officer, had decided to remain in the United States Army and fight for the Union. His father wrote him:

> Bath County, Virginia
> May 13, 1861

Sir—

I am *overwhelmed* by the position you have taken. It is the bitterest cup that has touched my lips. You are surely *demented*. Your talk about loyalty to your oath is all stuff. Oh! how it makes my heart bleed to think that while Virginians are rallying to the defense of her firesides and her homes, that my son is found playing the part of Benedict Arnold. . . . If you carry out the purpose you have avowed, no matter what may be the result, you will never be permitted to revisit your native land *but to die*. You should be hung before you could get 20 miles within the border of Virginia. . . . All your brothers and even your father, whose years would exempt him, will be in the fight. If you fight for the North your name shall be stricken from the family records, and only remembered in connection with your treachery to the country that gave you birth. . . .

> Your Father

In spite of his father's letter, William Terrill decided to fight for the Stars and Stripes.

In Virginia, Jefferson Davis, a West Point graduate who had been chosen as President of the Confederacy, was working hard to smooth out the confusion. Davis had served as a colonel in the old army, as a United States senator, and as Secretary of War for President Franklin Pierce. His experience was helping him arm the new country faster than the North.

From his offices in Richmond, the lean-cut Davis could see the throngs. Nearly everyone on the street wore a uniform of Confederate gray or butternut, a brown homespun cloth. Now a brass band marched down the street to aid in recruiting. The crowd cheered and many sang to the music

> *Oh, I wish I was in the land ob cotton,*
> *Old times dar are not forgotten,*
> *Look a-way look a-way, a-way,*
> *Dixie Land.*

The intense feeling in the South made Jeff Davis think his side could win. He called for 100,000 men to join the Confederate armed forces. They were to serve for a year. Davis knew that the outdoor life of the young Southerners fitted them for soldiering. He set up agencies in the Confederate War Department to get the Confederate Army under way. There was one soldier in the United States Army whom Davis was most anxious to obtain, Robert E. Lee.

Lee had served for thirty-two years in the old army and he had a brilliant record. He was a West Point graduate, and had served as the Superintendent of the Military Academy. Even as a cadet, Lee had been unusual, for he set a record which has never been equaled: he did not receive a single demerit in his four years in the Corps of Cadets.

As a cadet, young Lee had served under Colonel Sylvanus Thayer, the father of the Military Academy. There is no doubt that Lee's character was influenced by this great educator.

In the Mexican War, Robert Lee had been a scout behind the enemy lines. He was brave and daring. General Scott asked Lee to be on his staff, and there Lee saw how Scott handled large bodies of troops. Lee learned how a good commander takes care of his men.

When the war drums began to beat in 1861, General Scott recalled Lee from Texas and offered the command of the army in the field to him.

Colonel Lee faced a terrible decision. He had fought for the American flag and loved it. Slavery was not an issue in Lee's personal life, for his family had long ago freed their slaves. Here was the chance to realize his life's ambition to be a general in the United States Army. *But* Virginia, his state, had withdrawn from the Union. Virginia was his home. Could he fight against his home state and his relatives? After a hard inner struggle, Robert E. Lee resigned from the United States Army.

Scott felt bad. He had once said that Lee's life was so valuable to the country that it should be insured for $5,000,000. Scott knew that Colonel Lee would be the greatest military commander in America.

Chapter 4

ON TO RICHMOND!

PEOPLE in the North talked excitedly of how to stop the withdrawal of the Southern states. "On to Richmond!" they cried. "Let's capture Jeff Davis." Horace Greeley, the editor of the New York *Tribune*, urged Abe Lincoln to act fast. Something had to be done. *"On to Richmond!"* became the North's slogan. The capture of Richmond, the new capital of the Confederacy, appeared to be the answer to their problem.

Old General Scott's idea of sending an army down the Mississippi River Valley and then attacking the Confederates in Virginia seemed unnecessarily slow. His warning against a direct attack against the Confederate capital in Richmond was ignored. The Union officials wanted to get going, and fast.

But there were many obstacles. The Union War Department was bogged down under a mountain of paperwork. The clerical staff could not begin to handle all the details. Enterprising individuals raised regiments, then demanded commissions as colonels and generals. Such men usually had no military experience, and in war inexperienced leaders cost lives.

There were excellent leaders in the regular army, but many would be needed on the frontier.

At the start, the Federal Army suffered by doing business with dishonest contractors, men who were interested only in profit. These men sold the army shoes that fell to pieces in the rain, overshoes that rotted, blankets that were threadbare, a poor grade of salt meat, and wormy, hard crackers called "hardtack."

The system of recruiting was a mess. To speed enlistments, each man sworn in received $300. This caused trouble. Men without character ("bounty jumpers," they were called) would enlist in one unit, get their $300 bounty, desert, enlist in another unit, and collect another bonus. The *Official Records* tell of a man who did this thirty-two times!

Many of the men who answered Abe Lincoln's call had never even fired a gun. The big job of whipping an army into shape was just beginning.

The South was having troubles, too. The Confederate War Department estimated that their soldiers would need 10,000 rifles, and men were sent to Europe to purchase them. The actual number needed was closer to a million.

In their enthusiasm to defend the South, leaders in almost every community formed companies and then reported with their men, expecting to be used at once. John B. Gordon, a young man living in the mountains where the states of Alabama, Georgia, and Tennessee meet, was elected captain of a company of mountaineers. His men loved horses and, as every man owned at least one horse, they decided to go to war as cavalry. When they offered their services they were told, "no cavalry needed," so they turned in their horses and marched as infantry toward Milledgeville, then the Georgia state capital. In Atlanta the message reached them, "Turn around and go home." But finally "The Raccoon Roughs," as they called themselves, found a place in the Confederate Army.

John Gordon, a real leader, became one of Robert E. Lee's

major generals and one of the great military commanders leading
Southern soldiers on the battlefields. He was a modest man who
possessed a fine brain and a sense of humor.

"The Raccoon Roughs" were like nearly all newly formed
military units on both sides. They were armed with any kind of
weapon they could find. This complicated the problem of ammunition supply and added to the confusion. The North, with
its large industries, was the first to solve this problem and issue
regulation weapons.

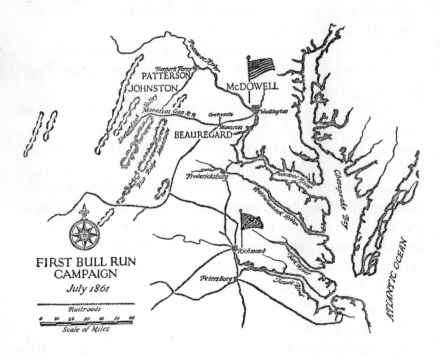

FIRST BULL RUN
CAMPAIGN
July 1861

Railroads
Scale of Miles

The South had one big advantage: the Yankees had to come
get them if they were to win. This meant that the Federal troops
would have to invade and overcome a brave people who were
fighting hard for their homes.

The Northern public demanded that President Lincoln order an attack. The press made fun of General Scott's idea of first training the army. And Lincoln feared that the enthusiasm of the Northern people for the war would give out. Some of his soldiers had been in the army all of three months and, as that was the term for which they had enlisted, they were already talking of going home.

To head his army, President Lincoln selected a fine-looking man, Irvin McDowell, who had recently been a major. General Scott, too old to take the field with the soldiers, gave the newly appointed Brigadier General McDowell the plan for the first battle.

"You attack and defeat the Rebels at Manassas. The Rebels also have troops over in the Shenandoah Valley. But do not worry about that. I have one of our generals, Robert Patterson, over there keeping them busy so they won't bother you."

Then Scott made sure General Patterson, an officer as old as himself, understood that he *must* keep the Confederates in front of him in the Shenandoah Valley. The Union plan hinged on Patterson's ability to do just that.

At Manassas, Virginia, a key railroad and road junction, on a sluggish stream called Bull Run, General Pierre Beauregard's green army labored to build breastworks. The Northern newspapers told Old Bory and the Confederates what was up. The headlines of the New York *Times* announced:

THE GREAT REBELLION

ADVANCE OF THE GRAND ARMY UNDER MCDOWELL

FIFTY-FIVE THOUSAND MEN

THE REBELS AT MANASSAS TO BE OVERWHELMED

There was no doubt but that there would be a fight at Manassas. In spite of their fears, their faulty preparations, and their untrained armies, both sides looked forward to victory. Both generals, McDowell and Old Bory, were confident they would win.

Chapter 5

THE BATTLE OF BULL RUN

GENERAL IRVIN McDOWELL rode his horse to a place where he could watch his soldiers march out of Washington and across the bridges over the Potomac River. It was a colorful sight. Bands played, flags and weapons caught the glint of the afternoon sun. When the musicians in the bands were not playing, the drummer boys picked up the step. The artillery cannons, drawn by horses, rumbled over the bridges. At the tail of the army came the covered supply wagons, many driven by Negroes.

Following Irvin McDowell's wagon train was a crowd of civilians in buggies and on horseback. Some were members of Congress. The civilians were in a gay mood, full of hope and confidence. All expected to see the Confederates beaten and chased back toward Richmond. The civilians carried their own food as though they were going to a fair. Some had champagne with which they would toast the victory. General McDowell was not overconfident. He wished his troops had more training.

On the day of the battle, President Lincoln left the White House to go to the War Department, for that was where the battle reports would come in. The President's wonderful sense of humor usually cheered those about him, as it would even in the Union's darkest hours, but at this moment the President and the officers of the War Department were on edge. *Would the Union Army defeat the Confederates?* No one could be certain of the answer.

Before the field telegraph train with General McDowell could be set up, a mounted messenger galloped to the War Department and delivered a despatch to President Lincoln. It read:

We are driving the enemy back toward Manassas. We have one officer and three men slightly wounded. We have captured a quantity of flour, fresh beef, entrenching tools, hospital furniture and baggage. . . .
Most respectfully, your obedient servant,

Irvin McDowell
Brigadier General

President Lincoln was delighted. The message appeared to be a good omen. The Union Army was off to a fine start.

But trouble lay ahead. Confederate spies in Washington had given Old Bory word of McDowell's plans. General Beauregard had wired President Davis in Richmond that he was certain General McDowell, with a huge army, was heading for Bull Run. President Davis telegraphed the Confederate Joe Johnston in the Shenandoah Valley:

"PUT YOUR TROOPS ON THE MANASSAS GAP RAILROAD AND MOVE QUICKLY TO THE AID OF GENERAL BEAUREGARD."

The jaunty General "Little Joe" Johnston, who had served with Lee at West Point and under General Scott in Mexico, had no trouble fooling old General Patterson. To get away from the Shenandoah, Johnston used a cavalry screen which hid his movements. The cavalry was commanded by a Confederate colonel, J. E. B. Stuart, who was to become one of the most daring Southern cavalrymen in the war.

One of Joe Johnston's officers was "Tom Fool" Jackson, as his students at the Virginia Military Institute called him. His real name was Thomas Jonathan Jackson and he was a brigadier general. He, too, was a West Point graduate who had served under old General Scott in Mexico.

On the trip to the railroad that would carry them to Bull Run, Jackson's men got wet fording a river. At night the question arose as to what men would stand guard. Jackson, a natural leader, saw how tired his men were, so he stood watch himself. He was strict, and at times his officers and men did not understand him, but they respected him because he was unselfish.

The first of the 9,000 Confederates from the Valley began to arrive in the rolling and wooded Bull Run country, at Manassas Junction, and were placed on the left of the line. The Union commander, McDowell, had no idea that Old Bory's men were being reinforced.

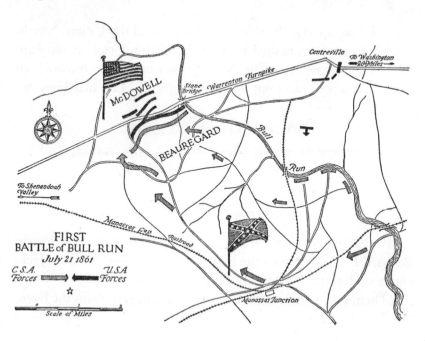

FIRST
BATTLE of BULL RUN
July 21 1861

C.S.A. Forces   U.S.A. Forces

Scale of Miles

Soldiers on both sides were nervous. Training, so important to teamwork, and the first step to victory, was utterly lacking. The Confederates behind their breastworks had cleared acres of ground so their cannons could fire effectively. The Confederates could see the bayonets of the oncoming Yankees glittering in the hot sun. They could see the many different kinds of uniforms the Northern Army was wearing.

The Yankee soldiers heard the bark of the Confederate cannons. They saw the shells burst, at first wide of their mark, now closer.

When the battle opened, there was confusion on the Union side because General McDowell tried to do everything himself. But Old Bory gave orders right and left, too, and soon forgot what orders he had given. Regardless of his muddled thinking, Old Bory had one great advantage: he knew, through the help of spies, that the Yankees would try to come around his left flank.

At the beginning, the tide of battle favored the Union. Northern newspapermen rushed to the field telegraph station and happily filed their reports. The New York *Times* quickly came out with an exciting account of the "victory." The headlines announced:

CRUSHING REBELLION

THE GREATEST BATTLE EVER FOUGHT ON THIS CONTINENT
FEARFUL CARNAGE ON BOTH SIDES

THE REBELS ROUTED

In the excitement of the fight, the Confederate General Barnard Bee rode across the battlefield to General Thomas Jackson and shouted, "They are beating us back!"

"Then, sir," said Jackson calmly, "we will give them the bayonet."

Many of Bee's men were frightened by the crash of the cannon balls and the rattle of musketry. They began to suffer casualties. The screams of the wounded were terrifying. General Bee's men showed signs of breaking for the rear. Bee waved his sword and pointed at Jackson. "There," Bee shouted, "stands Jackson like a stone wall." The men heard, and from then on Thomas Jackson was known by the nickname "Stonewall." A few moments later brave General Bee was mortally wounded.

The Union forces were having a hard time, for they were attacking piecemeal. That is, they did not attack together and hammer at the enemy with everything they had. This gave Beauregard time to put more of Joe Johnston's men, who were arriving on the railroad at Manassas Junction, into line on the left.

Near the end of the day the Union forces began to withdraw. When a Southern artillery battery fired into the tired Union troops crossing a bridge over a little stream near Centreville, the Union retreat turned into a panic.

Northern officers now had no control over their men. The civilian traffic rushed for Washington at top speed and tied up the roads. One Confederate said the Yankees ran so fast that their coattails stood out straight behind. It was a bad defeat for the Northerners. General McDowell, his heart in his boots, telegraphed President Lincoln:

THE VICTORY SEEMED COMPLETE. BUT OUR MEN, EXHAUSTED WITH FATIGUE AND THIRST AND CONFUSED BY FIRING INTO EACH OTHER, WERE ATTACKED BY THE ENEMY RESERVES AND DRIVEN BACK.

Later the general sent another despatch:

THE MEN HAVE THROWN AWAY THEIR HAVERSACKS IN THE BATTLE AND ARE WITHOUT FOOD. THEY HAVE EATEN NOTHING SINCE BREAKFAST. WE ARE OUT OF ARTILLERY AMMUNITION. THE LARGER PART OF THE MEN ARE A CONFUSED MOB, ENTIRELY DEMORALIZED.

President Jefferson Davis arrived at Manassas from Richmond on a special train. He had the pleasure of telegraphing his headquarters in Richmond:

WE HAVE WON A GLORIOUS THOUGH DEAR-BOUGHT VICTORY. NIGHT CLOSED ON THE ENEMY IN FULL FLIGHT AND CLOSELY PURSUED.

But Davis was in error. The Yankees were not pursued. The Confederates were tired, and taking over the spoils of the Union defeat—500 muskets, nine flags, twenty-eight cannons—plus the task of taking care of almost fifteen hundred prisoners, kept them from going after the retreating Union troops and gaining a full victory.

One man saw clearly the need of pursuit, Stonewall Jackson. He told Jeff Davis, "Give me 5,000 fresh men and I will be in Washington tomorrow." But Davis and Beauregard were more worried over the Confederate wounded than the escape of the Yankees. They did not listen to Stonewall.

The people of Washington came out of their homes and set up soup kitchens on the sidewalks to feed the downhearted soldiers, who were a pitiful sight. Many had thrown away their equipment and were lost from their officers.

The headlines in the New York *Times* the next day read:

DISASTER TO THE NATIONAL ARMY

RETREAT OF MCDOWELL'S COMMAND
90,000 REBELS IN THE FIELD

A PANIC AMONG TEAMSTERS AND CIVILIANS

When the news of the Battle of Bull Run came through to Richmond, the people were wild with excitement. They rang the church bells. General Lee, who had not seen the battle because he was on duty in the Confederate War Department as Davis' military adviser, sent his congratulations to Old Bory.

Generals Johnston and Beauregard thanked their troops in a long, high-sounding announcement.

The Northern people were depressed but not beaten. The day after the battle, Congress voted to ask for 500,000 volunteers.

President Lincoln now made up his mind to place a younger officer at the head of his army. He realized that Scott was too old and that Irvin McDowell had failed. Lincoln selected one of the most unusual generals ever to receive top command, George B. McClellan of Pennsylvania.

Chapter 6
THE PRESIDENTS AND
THEIR GENERALS

THERE was no doubt that President Lincoln had selected the right man to whip the down-and-almost-out Union Army into shape.

General George McClellan was thirty-five years old. He was smart about training troops, he was full of energy, and he had a fine background for the job. He had served as one of Scott's young officers in Mexico. Later he had helped survey the route for the Northern Pacific Railroad across the Cascade Range in the Northwest. The government had selected McClellan to go to southeastern Europe to observe the Crimean War, where he saw the Turkish, British, and French troops beat the Russians.

The square-shouldered George McClellan plunged into the task of reorganizing and training the Army of the Potomac, as it was soon called, with enthusiasm. Shortly the befuddled, disorganized mob began to look like an army. McClellan had his soldiers fortify Washington. There is an old army saying, "You can't fool the troops." As they toiled on gun positions, trenches, and other defense works, the soldiers realized that McClellan knew all about fortifications and training soldiers.

Discipline tightened; McClellan made both officers and men

behave. He improved the camps in which the men were living. He ordered drills and work with weapons. His officers and men loved him because he set the example and because he backed them up.

He also paid particular attention to the nonfighting parts of the army. He had the stretcher-bearers practice. He impressed on all officers that in battle the wounded must be removed rapidly from the battlefield and cared for properly.

There was one officer, Major Albert J. Meyer, who was interested in building a signal corps. McClellan encouraged him. Both officers saw the advantages of this new branch of the army. Albert Meyer developed a system whereby the Signal Corps could lay telegraph wire right behind advancing troops, and he taught his specialists how to signal with flags in the daytime and with torches at night.

Under McClellan the Army of the Potomac was beginning to look like a war machine.

The general was helped greatly in his work by Secretary of War Edward M. Stanton. McClellan and Stanton made a fine team. Stanton was determined that the Union Army would receive the best in food, clothing, equipment, arms, and ammunition. He demanded that contractors be square with the government. The discovery of a crooked contract made him furious.

Everyone began to sing General McClellan's praises. People called him "The Young Napoleon."

George McClellan gloried in this recognition and his vanity became a great fault. When photographers took his picture, the short, stocky general readily posed, with a hand thrust into the blouse of his uniform—a pose that Napoleon, the great French leader, had used. People made so much over General McClellan's fine work that he began to think of himself as superior even to President Lincoln.

One afternoon Lincoln went to McClellan's house to see the

general. George McClellan was not in, so President Lincoln waited. When McClellan did enter, he swept past the room in which the President was waiting and went upstairs. Lincoln sat patiently, waiting for the general to come down. But he did not appear. Finally Lincoln sent a servant to tell the general that he wanted to see him.

McClellan told the servant, "Tell the President I am tired and have gone to bed."

The President's advisers began to wonder why Lincoln stood for such rude treatment. Lincoln said, "I would hold McClellan's horse if it would help win the war."

After several months of hard work by McClellan and Stanton, Lincoln thought the army was ready to fight. General McClellan now had 200,000 men, probably the greatest army the world had ever seen.

But McClellan was not anxious to fight. He had been getting secret reports from behind the enemy lines from Allan Pinkerton, founder of the famous Pinkerton Detective Agency, and the detective convinced him that the Confederates had more than 126,000 men. As it turned out, Pinkerton was wrong.

George McClellan's second great fault, overcautiousness, began to govern him. He did not want to go into enemy territory with his army, great though it was, unless he had more men. He knew he would have to leave men to defend Washington, and others would get sick or could not fight for some reason. To cautious McClellan, the odds appeared to be in favor of the Confederates.

The President urged McClellan to go into Virginia and attack. But McClellan said he needed more men and, besides, the winter was making the roads bad.

While Abe Lincoln was wondering how to get McClellan started, he had trouble with another one of his generals, John C. Frémont. Frémont, known as The Pathfinder, was a dashing figure. Everyone knew him. He had explored the Rocky Mountains with the famous scout Kit Carson, and his leadership was well established in California. Now, as one of Lincoln's generals, Frémont began freeing slaves in Missouri, one of the border states.

President Lincoln tried to back up his generals, but he could not back up this sudden move of Frémont's. Lincoln wanted to free the slaves in the South when it would help the cause of the Union. "And that time has not arrived," Lincoln said.

Time was flying. Maybe England or France would come to the aid of the South. Lincoln tried every way he knew to get General McClellan to move, but no luck. The President met with excuse after excuse. So Lincoln put out what he called "Special War Order Number 1." It said that General McClellan would move upon the Confederate railroad at Manassas Junction before the twenty-second day of February.

The Young Napoleon was upset when he got this order. He explained to the President that it would be much better to place the army on ships and sail down Chesapeake Bay, landing on the tip of Virginia's great peninsula and from there striking at Richmond.

Lincoln patiently approved, instead of insisting on War Order Number 1. The President had but one thought. He would excuse anything if the North could win and the Union be put back together again.

In Richmond, President Jeff Davis had as many troubles as Abe Lincoln. Old Bory, the hero of Fort Sumter and Bull Run, was hard to control and insisted on having his own way. General Joseph E. Johnston, also a popular hero, argued bitterly with President Davis over rank. Joe Johnston was fourth on the list of Confederate generals. He thought he should be number one. And both Beauregard and Johnston wanted more soldiers.

A Confederate brigadier general by the name of William Whiting sent an angry telegram to President Davis: "What are they sending me unarmed and new regiments for? Don't want them. They will only be in the way. I want reinforcements, not recruits."

The Southern generals expected too much of President Jeff Davis and the new government. They wanted supplies of every kind and they expected Davis to furnish them and be quick about it. It was a difficult situation. The South had almost no resources except its people and a great desire for victory.

Chapter 7

FIRST FIGHT OF THE IRONCLADS

THERE was a tough-looking man-of-war lying off the tip of Virginia's peninsula waiting for McClellan's army.

Lieutenant John M. Brooke, an officer of the old United States Navy, now wearing Confederate gray, had the idea of raising a sunken ship and making her into the world's first ironclad. He covered the sides of the ship with thick iron plate sloping upward so enemy cannon balls would not strike her squarely. Her prow was equipped with a sharp iron ram and she mounted ten heavy guns. The Southerners christened her the *Virginia*. The North called her by her original name, the *Merrimac*.

The telegraph clattered in the War Department in Washington giving the news that the Confederates had a new type of war vessel capable of destroying every wooden ship afloat. There was great excitement. It looked as if General McClellan's move down the Potomac and Chesapeake Bay would be canceled. There was also concern for the safety of every ship in the United States Navy.

The Confederates aboard the *Virginia* did not wait long to fight. The new ship attacked two United States men-of-war, the *Cumberland* and the *Congress*, mounting a total of eighty guns.

35

When the two United States vessels opened fire, their crews were amazed to see the one-hundred-and-eighty-pound cannon balls roll off the armor plate of the Confederate ship like peas.

The *Virginia* rammed the *Cumberland*, raking her from end to end. The United States ship went down, carrying many brave sailors with her. The *Congress* tried to escape the iron-plated monster but could not and surrendered. Commodore Franklin Buchanan, Confederate States Navy, brought his ironclad alongside, removed the wounded from the United States ship, and set her afire.

Buchanan saw the United States frigate *Minnesota* near Fort Monroe at the tip of the peninsula. He would attack in the morning. But at daybreak a strange-looking ship steamed out from behind the *Minnesota*.

"What in the world is that?" asked a sailor on the *Virginia*.

"Looks like a cheesebox on a raft," said another.

"Or a round stump on a plank," observed a third.

Commodore Buchanan examined the odd-looking craft through his spyglass. He ordered breakfast served to his 260 Southern sailors, then steamed for the newcomer.

The name of the small ship was the *Monitor*, a name soon to be discussed in every port in the world.

The *Monitor* was an experiment. She had been invented by John Ericsson, a Swedish-American who had come to New York to build ships for the United States Navy. Officials in Washington had forgotten about Ericsson and his *Monitor*.

Ericsson's strange craft carried only two cannons. They were mounted in a small tower in the middle of the ship. To shunt enemy cannon balls away, Ericsson designed the tower so it would turn by the ship's machinery. A good idea, but it made it difficult for the men inside the turret, or tower, to fire the guns. The "cheesebox on the raft" was commanded by Lieutenant

John L. Worden, United States Navy, and he had fifty-seven Federal seamen in the ship's company.

The two ironclads started to fight. The heavy cannon balls bounced off the sides of both ships. The captains brought the ships closer—so close they were touching. The gunners on both ships worked as hard as they could. "Fire faster!" was the command. Both crews were under great strain. Each wondered if their ship would stand up under such cannonading.

For six hours the bombardment went on.

The *Virginia* tried a number of times to ram the *Monitor* but the *Virginia's* iron ram was damaged, and the smaller ship answered her rudder faster and could get out of the way. The crews were wringing wet with sweat and were black from the powder. Many were bleeding from the nose and ears—a result of the concussion of the cannon balls at such close quarters. Lieutenant Wordon had been looking out of a sighthole, or slit, when a cannon from the *Virginia*, ten yards away, fired, a shot striking the sighthole. It blinded him.

The *Virginia* began to leak, so she withdrew, still firing. She steamed toward her base in Norfolk.

The United States ship *Monitor* was badly battered but could have continued fighting when the battle ended.

President Lincoln and his cabinet breathed sighs of relief when the word came in about what John Ericsson's "iron cheesebox" had accomplished.

There was also great happiness in the South. Many Confederates thought the *Virginia* would be repaired and would sail north and reduce New York City to ashes.

The battle had great effect throughout the world. Foreign navies began immediately to scrap the wooden ships of war that had ruled the seven seas for centuries.

The two ironclads did not fight again. When the Confederates in Norfolk were called to abandon Norfolk and come to the defense of Richmond, the *Virginia* was left without a home port. She had no place from which to receive supplies. It was a sad day for the Confederacy when the proud *Virginia* steamed up the James River until she grounded and was set afire by her crew. The captain and his men did this because they did not want the Federals to capture her.

The U.S.S. *Monitor* came to a watery end en route to Charleston, South Carolina. She was traveling with the powerful sidewheeler, *Rhode Island*, when a hurricane from the West Indies crashed against them. The *Monitor*, never a good sailor, now battled for her life. When the seas got higher, tons of water smashed aboard the "cheesebox." At midnight, during the high point of the storm, the *Monitor* foundered. The *Rhode Island* managed to take off part of the crew, but the gale was too much and the fighting ship took sixteen brave men to the bottom.

Chapter 8

THE PENINSULAR CAMPAIGN

A YOUNG lieutenant of Confederate cavalry, on watch in a hickory tree, stared through his field glasses at the string of barges five hundred yards offshore. The tug, towing the flotilla on Chesapeake Bay, puffed toward Fortress Monroe. Two Union gunboats hovered about like hens protecting chicks.

The scout in the tree called to other scouts resting beside their horses in a pine thicket, "The gunboats are not going back up the bay. My guess is that this is the last of McClellan's army."

From the pines came an answering drawl: "Sure hope so. Just totaled up our notes. Countin' these barges, we've sent word to the telegraph office that the Yankees have brought down the bay a total of one hundred and thirteen steamers, a hundred and eighty-eight schooners, and eighty-eight barges. I figure Gen'ral McClellan must have more than a hundred thousand men. His army way outnumbers ours."

At the Richmond end of the telegraph line President Jeff Davis was worried. He had a thin line of men in trenches across the peninsula at Yorktown; 40,000 more guarded Richmond, and that was all on hand to face the tremendous Federal Army.

Confederate spies watched McClellan's army lumber away

from Fortress Monroe. It was obvious that his men were better trained than they were a year ago at Bull Run.

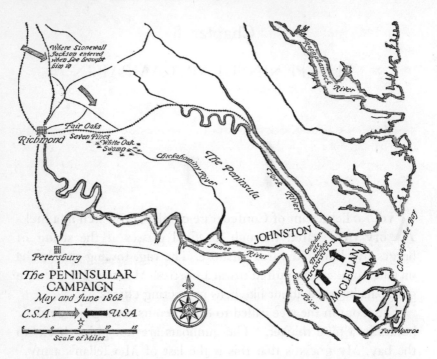

Where Stonewall Jackson entered when Lee brought him to

Fair Oaks
Seven Pines
Richmond
White Oak Swamp

Chickahominy River

The Peninsula

York River

Rappahannock River

JOHNSTON

Confederate Trenches

MCCLELLAN

Chesapeake Bay

Petersburg
The PENINSULAR
CAMPAIGN
May and June 1862
C.S.A. ▸▸▸   ◂◂◂ U.S.A.
0   5   10   15
Scale of Miles

James River

James River

Fort Monroe

The stocky George McClellan ("The Young Napoleon") rode forward under the protection of Union cavalry to scout the Confederate fortifications at Yorktown. *Here is warfare just like the textbooks,* he thought. *I'll have the men dig zigzag approach trenches toward the rebels, so that when I order the attack my men won't have far to go to the Confederate works. Good! Fewer men get killed in siege warfare than they do fighting in open country.*

This was true, but besieging an enemy is the slowest kind of fighting. The time consumed by McClellan's army in preparing trenches and bringing up siege equipment gave Jeff Davis time to get soldiers for the defense of Richmond.

For one whole month McClellan's 100,000 soldiers labored in front of Yorktown to besiege 15,000 Confederates. Their heavy guns were monsters. They weighed many tons and fired two-hundred-pound cannon balls. It took great labor to get the cannons into position, and some of his men were irked by the slow tactics. When the colonel of the 3rd Vermont found that the Confederates opposite him had gone to the rear to cut wood, he ordered a charge.

Back came the Confederate infantry. The bloodcurdling Rebel yell sounded through the woods, but the Vermonters did not scare easily. They answered with a yell of their own, "*Hoo-ray! Hoo-ray! Hoo-ray!*" The Rebel yell sounded as though the men were yelling on a raccoon or fox hunt. It sounded, "Who—*who—ey!* Who—*who—ey!* Who-*who-ey!*" The last two syllables of the Rebel yell were high-pitched and long.

The Confederates and Green Mountain Men crashed head on. Out marched the brother regiment to the Vermonters, the 6th Vermont, to help the 3rd. "Guide on the colors!" shouted the officers of the 6th.

For a while it looked as if the Vermonters would win, but George McClellan decided the fight was too risky, so he called it off and ordered his two regiments back into the Union lines.

At the end of the month the Young Napoleon decided that, by the "rules" of siege warfare, the time had come to get out of the approach trenches and fight. But the Confederates spoiled everything by leaving their fortifications and withdrawing toward Richmond.

General McClellan followed. He was in a harassed state of mind, for his intelligence chief, Allan Pinkerton, reported that General Joe Johnston now guarded Richmond with more than one hundred thousand Confederates. This was a great exaggeration, but McClellan did not check it. He wired Lincoln, "I need reinforcements badly."

Abe Lincoln sent word to a Federal army under Irvin Mc-Dowell, which was sixty-five miles north of Richmond, to be ready to march to help McClellan. This was real danger for the Confederates, for if the two armies attacked at the same time the gray armies would be in a vise.

When he saw the Confederates had left their fortifications at Yorktown, McClellan snailed forward. The roads were muddy and with every rain the muck got deeper. Wagons and cannons mired down; the animals pulling them were exhausted.

Conditions were even worse for the Confederates. They had no bread, no coffee, no hardtack, no flour, no sugar, and no change of dry uniforms. But their rear guard fought the Yankees every step of the way. The Southerners buried shells in mudholes and fused them so they would explode when the Yankees walked on them. When the Confederate general Old Pete Longstreet heard of this he objected, for he did not think this was a proper way to wage war.

During the Confederate retreat Colonel John Gordon (formerly of The Raccoon Roughs) found a young Southern soldier by the roadside. The boy's shoes were worn out and his feet were sore. Colonel Gordon dismounted from his horse and put the boy in the saddle.

The young soldier grinned. He took off his black slouch hat and waved it at his company, slogging it up the muddy road. "Attention, men!" cried the boy. "I'm bidding you farewell. I want you to know I am sorry for you. I was poor once myself."

The column laughed as they pushed on over the muddy roads and through the swamps. Close behind them pressed the men in blue. "Bluebirds," the Southerners called them.

The people in Richmond were nervous. Everyone in the city knew that the tremendous Union Army was getting nearer and nearer.

General Lee and President Davis were greatly concerned about Irvin McDowell's army to the north. To keep it away, Robert E. Lee thought up the idea of ordering Stonewall Jackson, in the Shenandoah Valley, to march to the north as if he were going to attack Washington.

When Lincoln heard of this he told General McDowell not to go to help McClellan but to strike for the Valley and try to get behind Jackson. Lincoln hoped to trap Stonewall Jackson in this way. This did not work, for McDowell was too slow.

Now McClellan's army had only ten miles to go to reach Richmond. It was a grim time. Some Confederate soldiers deserted. The Southern authorities rounded up many of these men and branded their backs with a red-hot iron, burning a capital D in their flesh.

When the Union troops were seven miles away, General Joe Johnston, in command of the Confederate Army, ordered his 85,000 men to attack.

McClellan's spies zoomed this number to 102,500. The Young Napoleon wired Lincoln that he needed more soldiers *at once*, and said he would die with his boots on.

President Lincoln was so worried he got aboard a special train and traveled to West Point, New York, to see old General Scott. The aged general pointed out that General McDowell's army was not in position to guard Washington nor to assist McClellan. The general's other views also helped the President.

Back at Richmond, Little Joe Johnston decided that his Confederate Army had retreated far enough, so he ordered an attack at Seven Pines. It was close-in fighting of the hardest kind. Sharpshooters on both sides were on the lookout for generals and colonels. They had learned that these men usually were on horseback. One Union rifleman drew a bead on Lieutenant General Wade Hampton, of South Carolina, and squeezed the trigger.

The general was hit in the foot. Hampton, an inspiring leader, would not get off his horse. He sent for a doctor and had him dress the wound while he sat on his mount under fire.

Another Confederate general received a musket ball through the shoulder. While those about him rushed to give him first aid, a shell burst overhead and the general received a slash in the chest. The wounded man was General Joe Johnston, the Confederate commander.

When Davis heard that Johnston was wounded, he placed General Robert E. Lee in command.

Part of this battle was fought in White Oak Swamp. Conditions were bad. Cannoneers worked at their guns, up to their waists in water. Two days later, at the end of the Battle of Seven Pines, there was a truce so both sides could get their dead and wounded out of the swamp. Eleven thousand men had died.

Several days after the Battle of Seven Pines, which both sides claimed to have won, a young brigadier general of Confederate cavalry rode up to General Lee and dismounted. In the horseman's hat was an ostrich plume. His gloves were yellow buckskin. A tasseled yellow sash encircled his waist. A red rose was thrust in a buttonhole of his short gray jacket. On his feet were golden spurs. He wore both saber and pistol. In addition to his striking uniform, the young general sported a thick mustache and a wide red beard. He was five feet ten inches tall and his sturdy frame still bore the effects of his training at West Point. Behind him, sitting on a sorrel horse, with a banjo strung over his shoulder, was Joseph Sweeney, the general's friend and personal musician. The dashing general, "Jeb" Stuart, had an unusual idea which he explained to General Lee.

"The Yankees," said Stuart, "can be circled by cavalry. Let me take twelve hundred men and raid them."

Lee approved. When Stuart's bugler sounded "Boots and Saddles," the men climbed on their horses. With them was a battery of artillery commanded by Captain John Pelham, one of the best artillerymen in the Southern Army.

Jeb Stuart led his men behind McClellan's army.

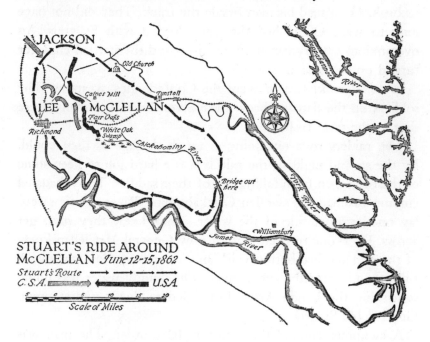

STUART'S RIDE AROUND McCLELLAN *June 12-15, 1862*

At three o'clock in the morning at Old Church, Virginia, his advance guard ran into Yankee cavalrymen. The Southerners drew sabers and charged. For a few moments it was a hot battle. Stuart gathered a number of prisoners and his column clattered on. Not far away they discovered a Federal camp which they set afire, burning $7,000,000 worth of supplies.

The column continued, although horses and men were tiring. Jeb Stuart had his leaders pass the word down the galloping column, telling his men if they fell behind they faced capture or death.

Near Tunstall's Station they overtook a Federal ordnance wagon loaded with Colt revolvers and canteens. The raiders helped themselves. At the station they dismounted and worked feverishly to tear up railroad tracks and telegraph lines. Soon after the work started they heard a train whistle. Jeb ordered an ambush. He placed his men beside the track. They did not have long to wait. On rushed the train, loaded with Federals. An overanxious cavalryman fired his pistol and the startled engineer turned on full steam.

Crack! Crack! Crack! went the Confederates' weapons. The soldiers on the flatcars threw themselves down, but many were shot as the train rushed by.

The raiders rode on, doing as much damage as they could. By the second night of the raid it was a hard job to keep some of the tired men from falling out of their saddles. The exhausted column reached the swollen Chickahominy River. Their safety lay on the other side of the water. They knew they *must* get across. Everyone realized that by now General McClellan knew of the raid and had both cavalry and infantry in close pursuit. A full moon lighted the angry river. The muddy water was doing something the Union Army had failed to do. It was stopping General Jeb Stuart.

A swimmer entered the water at Jeb's order. The man was swept downstream by the current. It was obvious that only the strongest swimmers and the best horses could get across. Jeb ordered trees felled in the hope of making a bridge, but the trees were too short. A scout returned from a visit downstream. He reported that a mile down the river was part of an old bridge. Jeb Stuart gave the job of rebuilding the bridge to Captain Redmond Burke.

Burke worked his men hard, and the bridge slowly began to take shape. After the Confederate raiders crossed it they set it afire. Ten minutes later Yankee cavalry rode up. Stuart had ridden safely around McClellan.

The entire Southern Army rejoiced. Jeb Stuart had secured

information for General Lee as to weaknesses in the Yankee lines, and he had burned valuable supplies. Only one Confederate had died and 165 Union men were taken prisoner. Stuart must have chuckled inwardly, for he had outwitted General Philip St. George Cooke, the Federal cavalry commander who was his father-in-law.

Shortly after Jeb Stuart made his famous ride around McClellan, rumors raced through the Confederate Army that Stonewall Jackson was coming from the Valley to help fight the Yankees. Lee went over his plan with his generals. He could place Stonewall Jackson's men on the left of the battle line.

But Stonewall Jackson did not put on a lightning attack as he had in the Shenandoah Valley and at Bull Run. This time he let his tired men rest.

In the fighting known as "The Seven Days," twenty-one regiments of Confederates marched straight into the Union positions near Beaver Dam Creek. The Union forces were on the high ground above a steep valley, lined with underbrush and thick woods. The Federal batteries were in position as Jackson advanced. The cannons took their toll: Stonewall Jackson left 2,000 dead and wounded on the banks of the stream.

On the Union side, the 8th Cavalry Regiment, Illinois Volunteers, was in reserve. Colonel John F. Farnsworth had each man standing "to horse"—at attention, holding the reins in a relaxed position, yet ready to mount in an instant. The Illinois men were surprised to see a dignified figure approaching. Many of them recognized the man. It was former Governor Wood, of Illinois. Governor Wood wore a black civilian suit and a high-crowned stovepipe hat, his snowy locks falling to his shoulders. The old man went with the colonel to inspect this fine regiment.

Suddenly an alarm came. The governor exchanged his tall hat for a slouch hat taken from the Confederates. The old gentleman buckled on a saber, pistol, and spurs. The men cheered as Governor Wood fought alongside them.

At Gaines' Mill, the color-bearer of this regiment, "Little Boy" Ryan, suffered the same fate as many, many color-bearers on both sides. John Ryan, nineteen years old and six feet six inches tall, drew fire and was badly wounded while carrying the colors. It was the custom to carry the flag to the keypoint of the battle-field. The colors were used for the men to "dress on"—that is, to line up on. The color-bearers were especially selected men, noted for their bravery and physique. Hundreds of them died in action; many more were wounded.

Back at the Federal headquarters General McClellan was desperate. The battle hung in the balance. He telegraphed frantically to Lincoln for more men. To the Secretary of War he sent an amazing message:

> ...IF YOU DO NOT KNOW NOW, THE GAME IS LOST. IF I
> SAVE THIS ARMY, I TELL YOU THAT I OWE NO THANKS TO
> YOU OR ANY PERSONS IN WASHINGTON. YOU HAVE DONE
> YOUR BEST TO SACRIFICE THIS ARMY.

When this message arrived in Washington, the men in the telegraph office thought it so bad that they cut out the worst part.

McClellan started to retreat to the James River. He called it "changing his base." By doing this he could readily receive supplies up the James River, and he was in position to try a new line of attack on Richmond. He sent an officer to Washington to explain to Lincoln that this "change of base" was one of the greatest feats ever carried on in face of an enemy.

President Lincoln traveled down Chesapeake Bay and up the James to find out for himself how the army was. He was surprised; the men did not look beaten.

The President returned to Washington and called in a general from the West, Henry W. (Old Brains) Halleck. Lincoln made him his general in chief. The President felt he needed a military expert to advise him what to do with McClellan and his army.

General Halleck came down to talk to McClellan. The Young Napoleon said that if he had 20,000 more men he would go up the James and attack Richmond from the south side. Halleck liked this idea, and he went back to tell Lincoln about it. But when Halleck arrived in Washington there was a new message from McClellan saying he needed *40,000 more* men if he was to attack.

This was too much for Lincoln. He ordered the Army of the Potomac withdrawn to the north, and the Peninsular campaign, a series of neglected opportunities for General McClellan, came to an end.

Chapter 9
STONEWALL JACKSON AND
HIS FOOT CAVALRY

W HEN Stonewall Jackson was a cadet at West Point, sixteen years before the war, he wrote in his notebook: *Avoid trifling conversation.*

Near the start of the fighting in the Shenandoah Valley, he planned a night attack against the Federals. He went over his plans carefully with his staff officers, making sure they understood exactly what he wanted. After the meeting, he invited his officers to ask questions. There was considerable discussion.

His troops made many errors in the battle. Stonewall Jackson said afterward, "I made a mistake in holding that conference before the fight. I will never hold another." And he never did. What others regarded as important conversation was "trifling" to Jackson. His staff officers did not like this trait of keeping battle plans from them. They explained to him they could do their jobs better if they knew his ideas. Stonewall listened but kept his plans to himself.

He was not imposing to look at. He was not neat in dress, and his six-foot frame was often clothed in a dusty old uniform. But there was something about him that demanded attention. Perhaps it was his light-blue eyes. Those eyes gave him one of his nicknames, "Old Blue Light." At other times his men referred to him as "Stonewall," but as they grew to love him, they called him simply "Old Jack."

He did unusual things. After the First Battle of Bull Run, Stonewall sent a letter to his pastor back in Lexington, Virginia. The minister was delighted to receive it. He thought, *Here is news of the battle from one who knows.* The preacher ripped open the envelope. He was amazed to find no news of the battle. Instead, there were money and a note from Jackson saying he was enclosing a contribution for the Negro Sunday-school class he had taught before the war started.

Stonewall was extremely religious. The great Civil War historian, Douglas Southall Freeman, wrote, "Stonewall Jackson lived by the New Testament and fought by the Old." Jackson studied the Bible and had the Lord in mind constantly. His servant Jim said he could tell when there was to be a fight because General Jackson always got up several times the night before a battle to kneel down and pray to the Lord.

Stonewall's amazing campaigns in the Shenandoah Valley of Virginia have been studied by military students the world over, for they show what can be accomplished by a fast-moving army when the officer in command is a smart, forceful leader.

The ground over which Stonewall would maneuver and fight was of great concern to him. He had lived at the Virginia Military Institute for nine years before the war. He knew the beautiful Shenandoah Valley, which served as the granary of Virginia. When he realized this was where he would fight he decided he must know every detail of the Valley, so he sent for Major Jed Hotchkiss, map expert.

Stonewall said quietly to Hotchkiss, "I want you to make me a map from Harper's Ferry to Lexington. You can get the materials from Mister Pendleton. Good morning, sir."

Not only was Stonewall Jackson helped by the map the major

prepared, but he had a fine adjutant, young Lieutenant "Sandie" Pendleton. Pendleton's most trying job was to find out for the other staff officers what the close-mouthed Jackson would do next.

But the man who helped Stonewall the most was a daring cavalryman, Brigadier General Turner Ashby. Ashby, known as "The Knight of the Valley," was probably the greatest horseman in the Confederacy. His password was *"Follow Me!"*

Once, when Stonewall Jackson was on a hill watching two bodies of cavalry fight at close quarters, there was some discussion as to which cavalryman in the distance was Ashby. A staff officer looked through his field glasses and said, "Sir, Ashby is the one with the smoking pistol."

Ashby's younger brother, Richard, commanded one of Turner Ashby's companies. On one scouting party Richard's small group ran into the enemy and after a hard fight Richard fell from his horse wounded. The Yankees won the skirmish, and a Yankee soldier stood over Richard with his bayonet an inch from the Confederate's stomach.

"Are you a Secesh?"[1] asked the Yankee.

"Yes," said Richard.

The Yankee soldier lunged with his bayonet.

When General Turner Ashby heard of this he was wild. He formed a scouting party of eleven horsemen and cried, "Charge, men! At them with your Bowie knives!"

In this close-in battle Turner Ashby fired sixty-six bullets from his pistols. He was shot in the leg and when his horse was killed under him Ashby went down still firing. The Yankees were defeated in one of the fiercest small battles of the war. Ashby had avenged his brother. Later, he buried Richard with military honors.

[1] Secesh—slang for secessionist—one who believed that his state had the right to secede from the Union.

General Turner Ashby believed in the cavalryman's saying, "When two groups of enemies meet unexpectedly, the side that acts first wins." There was never any doubt about Ashby. He led the way to the enemy's lines, sitting on his white horse as if he were part of the animal.

He died in a charge at sunset, near the end of the Valley campaign. This was a terrible loss to Jackson and the "foot cavalry." Ashby's last words were characteristic of his idea of warfare: "Charge, Virginians, charge!"

Stonewall Jackson was fortunate in having Ashby. He was also fortunate in having Lee lay out the over-all idea of the famous Valley campaign. It was General Lee who decided that, if Jackson maneuvered in the Valley, Lincoln would not send more troops against Richmond. General Lee told Jackson what he wanted and Stonewall drew up three campaign plans which he showed to Lee. Lee wisely let Stonewall select his own plan and the campaign started.

The Federal leaders sent 70,000 men into the Valley. The greatest force Jackson had was 17,000, and often it was less.

The series of fights opened when Confederate scouts galloped up to Stonewall's headquarters and reported that the Union Army at the north end of the Valley was moving farther to the north. Jackson thought this would be a good time to surprise the Federals. He put his small force on the road and started north.

Today, when soldiers hike, they march as a close, well-knit unit. They are trained in this way so that when they are called on to fight the unit can go into action quickly. In the Civil War, troops on the march did not stay so close together. Jackson's troops were no exception. They were strung out on the roads of the Valley for miles.

"Close up, men!" Stonewall would say as he rode along with them. "Close up!"

Jackson marched his men forty-three miles to the north in two days. When they arrived at Kernstown, Virginia, Jackson took time to pray to the Lord. Then he ordered an attack on what he thought was the enemy's rear guard. It turned out to be a force of 9,000 men. Jackson had only 3,290 men!

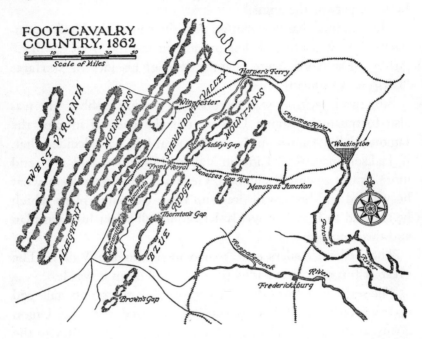

At first the fighting was even. Then the larger Union force began to win. One of Jackson's generals, Richard Garnett, ordered the famous "Stonewall Brigade"—the men who stood like a stone wall at Bull Run—to retreat. When Jackson heard of this he was furious. He was even angrier when the casualties were totaled up. He had lost 700 men. He thought that if Garnett had fought harder, fewer men would have died. He never forgave Garnett.

At this time General Lee helped Stonewall by sending him more troops under an officer who had had success in the West fighting Indians. This general was a strange-looking man. He had a bald head, scraggly whiskers, an eagle beak of a nose, and a high-pitched, birdlike voice. His name was Dick Ewell, known as "Old Baldy."

With the reinforcements Ewell brought, Jackson moved to attack. He was smarting from his defeat.

Foot soldiers usually think they have done a day's march when they have hiked fifteen miles. A twenty-mile march is hard work, especially when you carry a weapon, ammunition, a blanket roll, canteen of water, rations, and a small cooking utensil. Jackson marched his "foot cavalry," as his men called themselves, twenty-five, thirty, even forty miles in twenty-four hours. The men took pride in this accomplishment under their great leader. Their marches became the talk of the world.

Once, in his hideout on wild Massanutten Mountain, Stonewall's scouts reported that there were 4,000 Federals camped near the present-day West Virginia line. He marched rapidly toward the enemy and scattered them.

Then an unusual thing happened. A regiment of the old "Stonewall Brigade" announced they were going home. They told their colonel their time was up. They had enlisted, they said, for one year only. The colonel argued, but the men were firm, so the colonel reported the affair to General Jackson.

"What is this but mutiny?" demanded Stonewall. "These men should be shot! Why hasn't it been done?"

General Jackson ordered the mutinous men rounded up and surrounded by armed men. He told the mutineers that they had the choice of being killed right then or staying and fighting the Yankees. The men promised to stay and to carry out Jackson's orders. That was the end of the mutiny.

Stonewall now took the "foot cavalry" back to the northern part of the Valley to attack Yankees. It was a rocky route part of the way, but he marched them sixty miles in three days.

The Union general, Nathaniel Banks, did not know that

Stonewall was approaching. The Confederate leader sent a mounted messenger to his assistant, Dick Ewell. ". . . I will try, through God's blessing, to get in General Banks' rear."

On the march to fight Banks, General Jackson surprised and wiped out 900 Federal soldiers at Front Royal who were guarding a pass through the Blue Ridge Mountains. Here Jackson's men got needed supplies.

General Banks decided that the time had come to move nearer Harper's Ferry, where he might be reinforced. Stonewall raced to cut him off. The famous foot cavalry attacked at Winchester, and Banks lost 2,500—Stonewall, 400. Stonewall Jackson's men took so many supplies from the Union general that the foot cavalry nicknamed him "Commissary" Banks.

When Stonewall found time after the battle, he wrote his wife expressing his regret that it had been necessary to fight on Sunday.

While the South rejoiced over Jackson's successes, the North smarted. The Federal generals were having no success defeating Stonewall, so President Lincoln tried his hand. He ordered Union forces to block various gaps in the Blue Ridge Mountains and set a trap for the foot cavalry. But Jackson and his men avoided the trap by making marches of thirty-six and thirty miles and, while getting out of the pitfall, defeated two Federal armies Lincoln had sent against them. When Union cavalrymen slashed at his rear guard, Stonewall Jackson trapped *them*. One of his officers, Colonel J. M. Patton, said he hated to see so many Union men killed.

"Why?" asked Jackson.

"Because they are such brave men, sir," replied Patton.

"Shoot them all," said Jackson tartly. "I do not wish them to be brave."

The Valley campaign now came to an end. Stonewall Jackson and his foot cavalry had attacked and defeated four Union armies and had kept them so occupied that they had been unable to fight Lee near Richmond.

Many Union soldiers found graves in the ridges and meadows of the Shenandoah, but there was no time for formal military funerals with a drummer boy up front beating time.

Chapter 10

MUSIC—BLUE AND GRAY

THE drummer boys on both sides had an amazing spirit. The story of William Heimke, drummer boy from France, is typical of the loyal enthusiasm of these valuable members of the Union and Confederate armies.

William Heimke had always lived in France. When he was fourteen he read about the Civil War, and the more he read the more he determined to serve on the Union side. One night William kissed his twin sister good-by and left home, carrying with him the money they had saved together. She, too, believed in the Union's cause.

On board ship, and especially when he landed at the Battery in New York City, William was thankful that his father had made him study English.

He wandered about the streets until he saw a sign:

GENERAL STEWART VAN VLIET
QUARTERMASTER DEPARTMENT

William's heart leaped. He hoped this was the same General Van Vliet who had visited the Heimkes in their home in Versailles, France. He climbed the steps of the building and waited for a chance to meet the general. The officer was surprised to see William again and asked the boy if his mother knew where he was.

"No-o-o," said William shakily.

The general frowned.

"I am sending you back home," he said.

"Then I will run away again and come back. I want to be a drummer boy. If you do not need drummers, I can play the fife."

General Van Vliet scratched his head. What to do with such a person?

The general arranged for William to be assigned to a fife-and-drum corps on Governors Island, in New York Harbor. He saw many battles as a musician in the 17th United States Infantry.

Most drummer boys were members of infantry regiments and as "infantry" they took part in the hottest of battles and in long marches. In battle they often carried messages from one commander to another, which was dangerous work. Not only was there a chance of being hit by a bullet or shell, there was ever the chance of being captured.

James M. Lurvey, of the 40th Massachusetts Volunteer Infantry Regiment, had a different experience. In battle, the drummers in his regiment were employed as stretcher-bearers. Lurvey was too small to carry the end of a stretcher, so the colonel told him that when the regiment fought he would be an orderly in a field surgical tent. This was grueling work for young Jim Lurvey. It took a steady nerve to see the surgeons operate on a badly wounded man. Sometimes Jim had to help hold the patients while the doctors worked. Young Lurvey stood it, and with no prior training. He steeled himself to his duty.

The 51st Alabama Partisan Rangers had their drummer boy, James W. Moore, aged thirteen, help take care of the horses when he was not beating his drum.

Another drummer, Joseph Clovese, was born a slave in Louisiana. He watched his chance and, when opportunity came, the young Negro made his escape and joined the Northern forces at Vicksburg. He had an instinct for rhythm, which made him a splendid drummer.

In the Bircher home in South St. Paul, Minnesota, there was unusual drama when William Bircher, aged fourteen, got the idea of enlisting. William's mother was firmly against this because she felt that fourteen was too young to serve in the army. William could not wait to grow up, so he ran away to the recruiting office in St. Paul.

"You are too young," the recruiting sergeant told William.

This was a great disappointment. On the hike back to South St. Paul, William got an idea. He told his father about the exciting things he had seen and heard in the recruiting office. Mr. Bircher listened. He loved the Union as much as his son. After a while the father got the notion that *he* would enlist and take his son along. That was exactly what William wanted. Two Birchers against the mother was too much, and Mrs. Bircher finally gave in.

Bircher and his son held up their hands in the recruiting office and took the oath. They were assigned to the 2d Minnesota Regiment. Young William wrote that the happiest day of his life was when he put on his blue uniform for the first time and received his drum.

Life was not easy for the drummers. They took turns going on duty as drummer-of-the-guard. This meant being up at 4 A.M. to beat the long roll at Reveille, and staying up late at night to tap the drum three times after the bugler on duty had played Lights Out, as a final signal for the camp to quiet down.

On marches, the drummer boys were expected to beat time hour after hour so the soldiers could keep in step. Hiking with a drum and a forty-pound pack was difficult. On hot days on the march green troops on both sides looked for chances to lighten their loads. When the officers were not looking, undisciplined troops threw away clothing, blankets, and ammunition. There is no record of a drummer boy ever throwing away his drum.

Sometimes a colonel would tell a drummer he could place his pack in one of the wagons that followed the soldiers. The canvas-topped wagons, known as the "trains," often did not put in an appearance when the troops halted for the night. Enemy action, or mud, made the trains unreliable. A drummer boy learned that it was better to carry his pack and always have it, rather than place it in the train and maybe not see it for several days.

The drummers were respected and popular. One Union general, John E. Wool, recognized the worth of a boy in combat. "General Robert E. Lee," General Wool said, "could whip the world with an army of boys, for boys make the best soldiers. They do not know the meaning of danger. They are not afraid."

But life was not all danger or work for the drummer boys. They had fun, too. The drummer boys in Union camps sometimes teased the cooks by beating time on the drum while the men chanted as they waited in line for their food:

> Beans for breakfa:
> Beans for dinner,
> Beans for supper,
> Beans, *beans*, BEANS!

Drums and bugle calls have been used by military men as signals since biblical times. By ordering the buglers to play certain calls, officers in the Civil War could cause the tents in their units to come down at the same time. They could cause the sick to walk to the hospital tent for treatment, the unit to attend church, the men to fall in ranks, to come to attention, to halt on the march, and so on. The cavalry prided itself on its jaunty "Boots and Saddles," a call that ordered the riders to mount their horses. Then there was the stirring "Call to Arms," and the blood-tingling "Charge."

One Union general, the fatherly Dan Butterfield, took a special interest in buglers and bugle calls. He noticed that, when troops of different brigades were in camp close together, the bugle calls from one unit often confused the men of a neighboring unit. So Dan Butterfield invented a "signature" for the calls of his brigade. When a bugler played a call, he ended it with this signature:

Dan, Dan, Dan, Butterfield, Butterfield.

The soldiers of the brigade often sang the words of the signature: *"Dan, Dan, Dan, Butterfield, Butterfield."* They had a parody on the call, but they never sang it when he was near, for they liked the old general.

Not only was this signature a convenience, but the men felt it was their very own. This bugle call was used by General Butterfield to rally his men in the fierce Battle of Gettysburg.

Butterfield's men and other soldiers often amused themselves by singing the words to Reveille as the buglers woke the camp at the break of day:

I can't get 'em up, I can't get 'em up, I can't get 'em up in the morning,
I can't get 'em up, I can't get 'em up, I can't get 'em up at all.
The corporal's worse than the private, the sergeant's worse than the corporal,
The lieutenant's worse than the sergeant, and the captain's worst of all.
I can't get 'em up, I can't get 'em up, I can't get 'em up in the morning,
I can't get 'em up, I can't get 'em up, I can't get 'em up at all.

General Butterfield listened night after night to the Union Put-out-the-lights Call. He did not like it, because it was not beautiful. During the Peninsular campaign he sent for Oliver W. Norton, of Springfield, Pennsylvania, the best bugler he had. The general took young Norton into his tent and had him listen while he whistled a new tune. The general had the musical notes of the new call written on the back of an envelope. Then Butterfield had the bugler play the call back to him on his trumpet. This went on for sometime until Norton played the call the way the general wanted it.

That night, when it was time to put out the lights, Bugler Norton blew Taps over the camp for the first time. The next morning buglers from other units came over to Butterfield's brigade to ask what the call was. Soon Taps became so popular that orders announced it was the official lights-out call of the army.

The mournful melody of Taps was played over General Butterfield's grave when he was buried after the war.

But not all the music in camp was mournful. Men on both sides enjoyed the minstrel song, "Old Dan Tucker." There are many verses. Here is one, and the chorus:

> Old Dan Tucker was a good old man,
> Washed his face in a fryin' pan,
> Had the toothache in his heel,
> Combed his hair with a wagon wheel.

Chorus:
> So get out de way, get out de way!
> Get out de way, Old Dan Tucker,
> You're too late to get your supper.

Many regiments had bands that played music at drill, at parade, in camp, and after battles. The officers of the 6th Wisconsin Volunteers placed soldiers in their band who were in need of discipline. When a man in this regiment was caught doing something he shouldn't have done the regiment roared, "Put him in the brass band!" This custom led to that band's being able to play only one piece, and when the band wheezed and tooted the soldiers thought it a great joke.

Chapter 11

U. S. GRANT AND THE TWO CONFEDERATE FORTS

THERE was no brass-band music reaching the ears of a clerk sitting on the porch of a store in the small town of Galena, Illinois, in 1861. Near the country store a teamster worked to make a mule pull a wagon out of a mudhole. The small man slouching on the bench thought, *I am just like that wagon, stuck in the mud.*

Strange things happen in war. Miles away from Galena, back of the Confederate battle lines, General Lee listened to General Ewell, the fighter with the birdlike voice and the eagle-beaked nose. Lee wanted to know what Ewell knew about the Yankee generals.

"Sir," said Ewell, "there was one West Pointer, I think in Missouri. I hope the Northern people will not find out about him. I mean Sam Grant. He was at West Point with me when I was a cadet. He is quick, clear-headed, and daring."

Ewell could have added that Sam Grant had a bulldog determination and a character that could not be shaken.

Sam Grant had done well in the Mexican War but he found that was soon forgotten. Peacetime army life had bored Sam and, when a colonel whom he did not like was placed over him, Grant had resigned from the army.

For seven years Grant tried farming, selling wood, and working in his father's leather business. It was difficult for him to earn a living. At forty he was hardly a success.

When the war started, thousands and thousands of men rushed to join the Union Army or the Navy. Sam Grant offered his services but he found he had become a man no one remembered. He knew General George McClellan, but the Young Napoleon could not bother about former Captain Grant. No one had time for the man who would play a principal role in saving the Union and who would become the eighteenth President of the United States.

Grant went from one army official to another. Finally he applied to Governor Richard Yates of Illinois. The governor listened. Many others had come to see him asking for important jobs in the war. The official was impressed by the small man with the blue eyes who wanted only a chance to fight.

So Grant got an opportunity. The governor commissioned him as a colonel commanding the 21st Illinois Infantry. This regiment was poorly disciplined; the men did just about as they pleased. Some wondered if Sam Grant could control this rowdy crowd, but with eleven hard years in the regular army behind him, Grant *knew* he could command men.

The first time he walked out in front of his new regiment, the men laughed. They jeered at the stocky fellow dressed in shabby civilian clothes. He looked like a joke. But the soldiers soon discovered that Grant was a leader who did everything he asked them to do and that he took care of them. The regiment improved, and before long Abraham Lincoln promoted Grant to brigadier general.

Sam's first big job was to lead his men in the country of the Tennessee and Cumberland rivers against two Confederate forts.

If he could take the two forts, the Union would gain, for Fort Henry would no longer block the waterway to Alabama, nor Fort Donelson guard the avenue to the important city of Nashville.

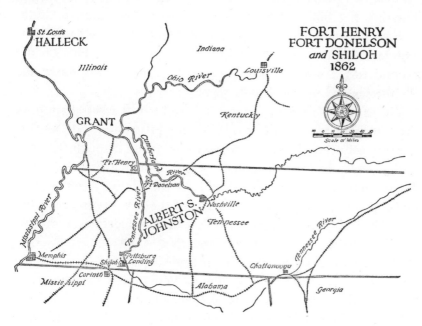

Grant thought out a plan and took it to General Halleck, who had not yet been called east by the President. "Old Brains" Halleck did not like the plan and said so in tart fashion. He was inexcusably rude to Grant.

Grant was crestfallen, but he did not give up. He was determined to take the forts although they were occupied by thousands of Confederates and the weather was bad. It was January, 1862.

In the attack against the forts, Grant received help from a graduate of the United States Naval Academy, Andrew Foote, who commanded gunboats on the Mississippi River. These two leaders had two things in common: they were unconcerned about themselves, and they were anxious to win for the Union.

The campaign to take Fort Henry was easy, for the Confederates ran up the white flag after little struggle. There was one bad incident when a cannon ball tore through the gunboat *Essex*, bursting her boiler and scalding many of her crew to death.

Few prisoners were taken at Fort Henry because the Southerners had fled to Fort Donelson. To help in the attack on the second fort, Admiral Foote's gunboats steamed back down the Tennessee and up the Cumberland.

Grant hiked his soldiers overland, and it was a hard march. A freezing rain fell and the roads became quagmires. The soldiers threw away their blankets to make the march through the mud easier, and paid for this at night when the temperature dropped below zero. Some froze to death. As the Union Army neared the fort, Grant added to the misery of the men by ordering "no fires" because he did not wish to alert the Confederates of the oncoming attack. He was determined to *win*.

The problem facing the Union leader was how to attack the huge, one-hundred-acre stronghold. While his men labored to get the artillery through the mud, General Grant took a regiment of cavalry and rode near the fort. He wanted to study the ground over which his men would fight. He saw at once the fort was well located. Because the ground sloped away from the fort, the men inside had excellent ground over which to shoot.

But there was a weakness, and Grant suspected it. He believed that of the three Confederate generals in Fort Donelson, only one was a stanch, last-ditch fighter. That man was Simon Bolivar Buckner of Kentucky. The other two, John Floyd and Gideon Pillow, would not be so determined when the pressure was on.

Just before the fight General Grant received a despatch from Old Brains Halleck ordering him to go back and fortify Fort Henry. But Grant went ahead. He did everything in his power to speed up the attack before the Confederates reinforced the men in the fort. General Halleck should have lost his nickname right then, because the important place to capture was the frowning stronghold on the hill, Fort Donelson.

The gunboats arrived, and the Confederates sent their cannon balls plunging down on the decks of the ships. The men-of-war returned shot for shot. The wooded countryside rang with the crash of battle.

The gunboats received a hard beating. Admiral Foote stood on his flagship, *St. Louis*, while only three hundred and fifty yards away Confederate cannoneers pumped sixty shots into the square-built vessel. One shell burst on the *St. Louis*, killing the pilot and wounding the man next to him, Flag Officer Foote.

The gunboats withdrew, leaving the Confederates in a great state of excitement. They thought they had won. General Floyd telegraphed General Lee in Richmond that it was a great victory for the South. But it was soon obvious that General Grant was not giving up.

Grant went aboard the flagship to see the wounded naval officer. Andrew Foote was hurt, but he had plenty of fight left. He suggested to the general that the soldiers lay siege to the fort. "I'll take the gunboats down-river for repairs and come back and help. We'll capture the fort," Foote said.

But this was too slow for Grant. He rode back through the woods, turning over several plans in his mind. Hearing the blood-curdling Rebel yell, he spurred his horse ahead and saw the Confederates coming out of the fort, shooting at the men in blue.

Grant was a cool man under fire. Some of his men became panicky and plunged through the swamps for the rear. Grant stopped them. He examined a captured Confederate soldier his men brought to him. The Confederate's knapsack was crammed with cooked bacon and corn bread.

Grant realized at once what the enemy was trying to do. He said in his matter-of-fact way, "These men are not attacking. They are carrying too much food for a day's attack. They are trying to escape."

The smart Union leader gave the command, "Fill your cartridge boxes quick and get in line. The enemy is trying to get away. We must stop him!"

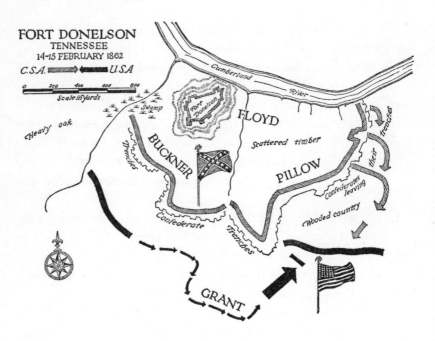

FORT DONELSON
TENNESSEE
14-15 FEBRUARY 1862
C.S.A. ━━━━▶◀━━━━ U.S.A

When the Confederate generals, Floyd and Pillow, saw the effort to leave the fort was a failure, they left their men and arranged for Grant's friend of his cadet days at West Point, General Buckner, to surrender. A Confederate cavalry leader in the fort, Colonel Forrest, cut his way out with many of his men. If Grant could have captured this fighter, he would have saved the Union much trouble.

Out of the fort came a flag of truce. Buckner asked Grant

what terms he would allow. Grant's note made his old friend
angry. It read:

Gen. S. B. Buckner,
Confed. Army.

Sir,
   ... No terms except unconditional and immediate surrender can
be accepted.
   I propose to move immediately upon your works.
Your obedient servant,
U. S. Grant
Brigadier General

Buckner sent a note to Grant calling him unchivalrous and un-
generous, but Buckner surrendered.

The capture of Forts Henry and Donelson was great news for
the North. There were celebrations everywhere throughout the
United States. Grant's reply to Buckner was quoted in Northern
newspapers. People said Grant's initials "U.S.G." stood for "Unconditional Surrender Grant."

President Lincoln was delighted. The twin victories opened
the two rivers, they split the Confederate lines across northern
Kentucky, and, what was better, Lincoln found a general who
could win and who did not ask for more men every time he
turned around.

Sam Grant took his victories modestly. It had been a hard
campaign. At Fort Donelson 510 Union soldiers had been killed,
but in the battles ahead such casualties would be considered small.

Chapter 12

SHILOH

MANY men died in the fierce Battle of Shiloh. It was the first battle in the War Between the States (which is the term the Southern people called the Civil War) in which the killed, wounded, and missing totaled as high as 23,000.

Shiloh is a tale of fighting in close quarters: in thickets, scrubby woods, underbrush, dark ravines, and along the muddy banks of a river.

The Confederates at Shiloh were commanded by a striking leader, General Albert Sidney Johnston. He was more than six feet tall, weighed one hundred and eighty pounds, and carried himself like an athlete. His square-trimmed mustache and high cheekbones gave him the clean look of a Scotsman.

Few leaders on either side could boast of a record like Albert Johnston's. He had been Secretary of War to the Republic of Texas, a colonel in the United States Cavalry, and a successful Indian fighter. When the Civil War started, the Secretary of War in Washington rushed a message to Johnston by telegraph and Pony Rider Express, offering him a top command in the Union Army. But Johnston preferred to fight for his adopted state, Texas. When President Davis received that news, he was delighted. He said Albert Johnston was worth 10,000 men.

General Johnston realized trouble lay ahead, for most of his Confederates were untrained. He gathered his men at Corinth, an important railroad station in North Mississippi.

Reports from scouts, spies, and Southern sympathizers informed him that General U. S. Grant had come up the Tennessee River, his transports protected by two gunboats. Thirty-three thousand Yankees were on the river ships.

As poorly trained as his Confederates were, General Johnston felt he must attack at once. He sent the Confederate headquarters in Richmond a telegram:

> OUR FORCES HERE ARE 40,000. EXPECT TO OFFER BATTLE NEAR PITTSBURG LANDING. HOPE TO FIGHT GRANT BEFORE GENERAL BUELL CAN JOIN HIM.

Johnston had the key to victory: defeat Grant before he could be reinforced by Buell's army, which was slogging down the roads from central Tennessee. This would require speed as well as fierce fighting.

There have been few marches like the twenty-two-mile hike of Johnston's army from Corinth to Pittsburg Landing on the Tennessee. The soldiers straggled all over the country. They shot at any game they saw, and many fired their guns to get target practice. The men were in a holiday mood. "Old Bory," who was under Albert Johnston at this time, felt certain so much noise would prevent the Yankees from being surprised. But Johnston decided the time had come to fight. He told his staff as they rode out of Corinth, "Gentlemen, tonight we will water our horses in the Tennessee River." The men reflected Johnston's enthusiasm. They wanted to kill Yankees.

The morning of Sunday April 6, 1862, was foggy. At half-past five the Federals crawled out of their new two-man tents.

The drummer boys and buglers sounded Reveille. After the rolls had been called, the men lit their fires and cooked their own breakfasts. Some prepared a dish called "hardtack pudding." It called for you to grind up your hardtack, add a little flour to make a stiff dough, roll it out, then cover it with stewed fruit— if you had any fruit—then wrap it in a cloth and boil it. The smoke from the hundreds of small fires hung low in the trees.

The sun cut through and the fog lifted. It was a grand spring morning. The men wondered if there would be church services in the log chapel not far from the Landing. The chapel was called Shiloh. It was too small to accommodate a large congregation, so the regimental and brigade chaplains would preach under the shade of the trees.

General William Tecumseh Sherman, a close friend of Grant's, came out of his tent. Sherman thought there was no danger. He had not ordered his men to fortify their camp, he had not even formed an outpost which could give warning of an approaching enemy.

Suddenly the Confederates burst through the woods. Thousands of their muskets barked. The attack had started. So had confusion.

The drummer boy of the 44th Indiana Volunteer Infantry grabbed his drum and beat the long roll. At the same time Union soldiers dashed through the camp of the 44th yelling, "You'll catch it! We're cut to pieces! The Rebels are coming!"

The Federals formed as best they could, but the officers as well as the men were untrained. Like the Confederates, the Union soldiers had elected their company officers and many were not qualified to command. A number of Union men had never fired their weapons.

When the bullets clipped off the branches of the trees, two Union colonels led their regiments hurriedly to the rear. They wanted no part of the battle. Private John Blake, of the 81st Ohio

Volunteer Infantry, said later that on his way to the rear he found a Union officer and two privates, from the same regiment, hiding in a hollow log.

Two thousand five hundred Union troops were surrounded. They surrendered. Approximately nine thousand others hid under the bluff on the riverbank. But many brave Union men stood fast and returned the fire of the Confederates. General Sherman organized his lines as best he could. Thickets and tangled ravines separated the units of both armies. Numerous small fights broke out in the dense woods. The battlefield was so thick with scrub growth that the best of trained troops would have had trouble keeping together.

The great poet, Stephen Vincent Benét, described such difficulty when he wrote "John Brown's Body": [1]

> If you take a flat map
> And move wooden blocks upon it ...
> The thing looks well, the blocks behave
>   as they should.
> The science of war is moving men like blocks.
>
>   . . .
>
> But it takes time to mold your men like blocks
> And flat maps turn into country where creeks
>   and gullies
> Hamper your wooden squares. They stick
>   in the brush. . . .

The thunder of the cannons was heard by General Grant, who was down the river twelve miles. He immediately placed his staff and horses aboard a steamer and headed for the battle.

Confederates from Louisiana were receiving fire from other Confederates because the blue uniforms of the men from Louisiana were mistaken for Union blue. The Louisianians turned their

[1] From *John Brown's Body*, copyright, 1927, 1928, by Stephen Vincent Benét, published by Rinehart & Company. (Copyright renewed, 1955, 1956.)

coats inside out, but the linings were white and they made excellent targets.

Over near a peach orchard, a sunken road a foot deep played an important part. General Prentiss and 3,000 Union soldiers lay down, sheltered by the banks of the road. Their aimed fire saved the men who had retreated to the riverbank. The Confederates called this sunken road the "Hornets' Nest."

In the peach orchard, the Federals were under heavy fire. The bullets zipping through the trees cut peach limbs, and petals and branches fell on the men below.

The steamer carrying General Grant puffed up to the landing. General Grant did his best to get the men under the riverbank to go back to their regiments, with varied success.

Because the range is short in woods, cannoneers on both sides loaded canister [2] into their field pieces. This is a vicious close-range weapon. The screams of the wounded rose above the crash of the artillery and rattle of musketry. Color-bearers waved their colors in the centers of their units as officers shouted commands.

Two gunboats got into position and their cannon balls crashed through the trees at the Confederates. On the left flank of the Confederate line the Texas Rangers rode up and dismounted. They handed their horses over to some of their men who acted as "horse-holders," then fought as infantry.

The generals were catching it as well as the men. General Sherman's horse went down, but shortly Sherman reappeared in the fight, his arm in a sling and his face bloody.

The Confederate advance was going too slowly to suit General Albert Johnston. He put his spurs against the flanks of his horse, "Fire-eater," and galloped to the center of a Tennessee regiment which was held up by the "Hornets' Nest."

---

[2] Canister—a round tin can made to fit in a gun. The can is filled with bullets and sometimes scrap iron. When the gun is fired, the bullets scatter like bird shot.

Johnston sat erect in his saddle. He drew his sword and pointed with it at the Yankees, shouting to his men, "They are stubborn! We must use the bayonet!"

The Confederates charged and the Union men withdrew. But the Confederates paid dearly, for General Johnston was hit. He said it was "only a scratch." When they lifted the general out of the saddle, they found an artery in his leg had been cut by a Minié ball.[3] He bled to death because those around him did not know how to apply a tourniquet.

General Beauregard now assumed command of the Southern side.

The first day of the terrible battle drew to a close with the Confederates in command of the field. The Southern cavalryman, Forrest, decided that he would scout out the Union lines. He dressed a number of brave men in Federal uniforms and sent them forward. Had these men been captured, they would have been hanged as spies. They accomplished their mission but they had bad news. They reported that thousands of Union men were being marched off the river boats to the beat of their drums, chanting, *"Buell! Buell! Buell!"*

Forrest told this to a Confederate general, but it made little impression.

The next day Buell's men in blue made the difference. The Confederates were beaten back. "Old Bory" himself seized the colors. He waved the Stars and Bars of the Confederacy and tried to rally his soldiers, but his men were outnumbered. They felt as though they were fighting an avalanche.

At four in the afternoon Old Bory withdrew his exhausted troops. They came out of the tangled growth and dragged back to Corinth. The Union Army was too tired to pursue.

Smoke drew slowly away from the fearful field of Shiloh. In

---

[3] Minié ball—a heavy lead projectile, about ¾ inch high and more than ½ inch thick, fired from a powerful musket.

the log chapel, surgeons labored to save as many wounded men as they could. Governor O. P. Morton of Indiana telegraphed the Secretary of War and got his permission to bring extra doctors to Shiloh and to take the wounded home on river boats.

Old Bory scratched out a wire to Richmond:

> ... THANKS TO THE ALMIGHTY, WE GAINED A COMPLETE VICTORY. ...

At the same time, Lincoln's Secretary of War announced that the Union had won.

Two things were certain: both sides had paid dearly in this battle, and the South had failed in its strike to wipe out the conquerors of Forts Henry and Donelson.

While this costly battle was being fought, the Union general, John Pope, with Foote's gunboats, attacked the heavily fortified Island No. 10 in the Mississippi River.

Here the Federals cut a canal in the swamps so the gunboats could pass behind the Confederate guns of the fort. The daring Commander Walke decided to take his Union gunboat *Carondelet* downstream past the batteries.

Walke selected a dark, stormy night. With a full head of steam, he steered the ironclad past the fortress. There were no searchlights, no navigation aids in the channel, and heavy Confederate guns were ready to blow the ship out of the water. But Walke got through.

Once below Island No. 10, the *Carondelet* blocked all relief and the 7,000 Confederate soldiers on the island surrendered.

Chapter 13

WAR ON THE WATER

THE Union was having more success at sea than on land.
Early in 1862, Lincoln aimed a combined army and navy
force at the North Carolina coast. This expedition, under Flag
Officer Gainsborough and General Burnside, captured the Confederate works on Albemarle Sound.

But not every expedition on the water was a Federal victory.
Benjamin F. Butler, the worst kind of political general, got the
idea that he could also send his soldiers to land on the North
Carolina coast. As a result of his poor planning, the Confederates
easily captured 300 brave men.

Lincoln had gotten the war on the water under way soon after
the Civil War started when he ordered 4,000 miles of Confederate coast line blockaded. This was a big job.

There were only forty-two good ships in the Union Navy
and they were scattered over a tremendous area. To get enough
ships to stop traffic in and out of Southern ports, the North
placed guns on almost every kind of craft. Even ferryboats were
used as navy ships.

President Lincoln knew the South would need supplies such
as ammunition, guns, clothing, medicines, paper, cooking utensils,

79

coffee, tea, and needles. His idea was to stop such supplies from coming into Southern harbors.

When the Northern warships took up their watch outside the Southern coastal cities, the first thing the South missed was salt. In the 1800's people depended upon salt to keep meat from spoiling. There was some salt in Florida, but it took a long haul to get it to people in Tennessee, Virginia, and other places.

President Davis hoped England and other countries would become angry at their loss of trade, caused by the blockade, and would go to war with the North over this. England almost declared war on the United States, but not over trade.

When President Davis sent two men, Mason and Slidell, as Southern ambassadors to London and Paris, the entire world was electrified because a Yankee man-of-war stopped the British mail packet, *Trent*, and arrested Mason and Slidell.

The British people were angry. They did not like having one of their ships stopped and searched, and for a few days it looked as though England might attack the North. But the United States released the two men and England stayed out of the fighting.

As the war went on, more ships were built. The blockade of the Southern coast became more effective, but at great cost to the Union. The Federal ships could not stay at sea indefinitely. Crews had to be rested, ships overhauled and refueled. The blockade continued in winter and in summer, in rough weather as well as calm.

When the bite of the blockade began to make itself felt, a daring group of Southerners went into a hair-raising business called blockade-running. This profession brought watery graves to Southern seamen who were unlucky or who sailed on slow ships.

The blockade runners built low-hulled, fast ships for their trade. They slipped quietly out of Southern harbors at night, their ships laden with cotton or other goods that would sell readily in foreign ports. The Union warships were alert to stop this and there were exciting chases.

Captain John Wilkinson was a daring blockade-runner. One dark night he sailed his ship to sea carrying a cargo of cotton, turpentine, and gold. When daylight came, Captain Wilkinson was startled to find a Yankee warship not far away, ready to swoop down for the kill.

It looked as though the Southerner would be caught. The men in the engine room could get no more steam out of the boiler. The Federal man-of-war steamed closer. Wilkinson called for his chief engineer.

"Take the cotton. Pour turpentine on it and stuff it into the boiler!"

The engineer knew this might cause the ship to catch fire, but he did it. The Southerner picked up speed and darted away from her pursuer. When his ship reached the Bahamas, Captain Wilkinson opened a keg of gold and doubled the pay of his crew.

Running the blockade was dangerous but it paid handsomely. The blockade-runner, *Banshee No. 2,* brought her owners more than three hundred and sixty thousand dollars on one trip.

The South made fun of the blockade at first. They said it was ineffective and that President Lincoln had made a costly mistake when he ordered it. However, prices went up, and in New Orleans business almost stopped.

But New Orleans had more to worry about in 1862 than the ships guarding her exit to the sea, for Admiral David Farragut had a Yankee fleet nearby in the Gulf of Mexico.

Farragut was a splendid officer of the old school. He had been a midshipman at the Naval Academy. He had fought in the War of 1812, against pirates, and against Mexico. He had a practical naval background gained by years at sea and was a natural leader with a winning smile. Because he had been born in Tennessee, he was not given an important assignment until 1862. But when the Union needed an experienced seaman to solve the problem of New Orleans, it called on David Farragut.

The task given him was not easy, for the mouth of the Mississippi was guarded by two forts, Jackson and St. Philip. A fort is a difficult thing for a naval vessel to attack. To slow up Union men-of-war coming upstream, so that gunners on shore could get a good chance to aim their cannons, the Confederates blocked the way by a line of old hulks which were firmly anchored.

The Federal fleet pounded the forts for five days and nights. On the fifth day Farragut's men were exhausted because they had been unable to sleep.

It was even worse for the men inside the forts.

Every once in a while the Confederates up the river would send down immense fire rafts made of wood. The rafts had been saturated with pitch and resin, then a torch was thrown on board. The Southerners hoped these rafts, which sent flames up a hundred feet into the air, would set the Yankee ships afire.

At a council of war some of Admiral Farragut's captains thought the fleet could not get by the shore batteries even though a channel had been made through the sunken hulks. Farragut listened, then ordered his fleet to advance at two in the morning.

Many fire rafts were pushed into the river and set afire. Their blaze lit up the night. A Southern tug pushed a flaming raft into the *Hartford*, Admiral Farragut's flagship. The rigging caught fire but she sunk the tug and got away from the raft. The Union ship, *Brooklyn*, moved directly in line of the guns of one of the forts and close to the flagship to protect her while she was fighting fire. It was a bold act and it saved the *Hartford*.

The ships got by the forts, after fighting several Confederate ships at close quarters, and steamed seventy miles upstream to New Orleans. The men in the Confederate forts now surrendered.

There was an angry mob waiting in New Orleans for the

Union Navy. Admiral Farragut put only two men ashore, Captain Ted Bailey and Lieutenant George Perkins. They walked coolly through the howling mob which threatened to kill them, and arrived at city hall, where they demanded the surrender of the city. They got it.

Three days later the Union political general, Benjamin Butler, and his men arrived to take over New Orleans. Butler became a hated person because of his crude ways.

Farragut left New Orleans and steamed up the Mississippi with no opposition except for some occasional rifle fire from Confederate sharpshooters on the banks. Baton Rouge and other cities up the river fell to Farragut's fleet.

His well-planned attack on New Orleans placed Admiral David Farragut as one of the great naval commanders in the world. The fall of New Orleans was thrilling news in the North, but the Confederates resolved to fight that much harder. The Union had won an important victory, but the war was far from over.

Chapter 14

SECOND BULL RUN AND
TROUBLE IN MARYLAND

A THOUSAND miles from New Orleans a confusing situation existed in the Union Army.

General McClellan, The Young Napoleon, was still on the Virginia Peninsula with his army. President Lincoln formed a new army in northern Virginia and made John Pope its general. When General McClellan heard of this he telegraphed "Old Brains" Halleck (who was now in Washington assisting the President) and asked if General Pope came under him. General McClellan also asked where General Pope's new army was. "Old Brains" sent a strange reply. He said he had no time for such "details." This amazing answer baffled General McClellan.

Lincoln added to the tangle by writing McClellan and asking what news he had of Pope. McClellan was glad to hear from the President, for this gave him an opportunity to give the President some advice. After he had done that, McClellan asked Lincoln for instructions.

Lincoln was cautious. He said that instructions should come from General Halleck. When McClellan put this problem to Halleck, "Old Brains" said that he was tired out.

This muddled situation gave General John Pope, the head of

Lincoln's new army, a chance to talk, and Pope loved to do just that. He told Abe he would do anything desired—including taking Richmond from the Confederates.

The new general was a striking-looking officer. He wore his uniform well and he made a great impression on anyone meeting him for the first time, but he was a strange character.

John Pope started by publishing an unusual order to his army. In it he bragged about his success at Island No. 10. He said he was used to being with people who always went forward. The soldiers did not like this. They thought he was belittling them.

But a greater fault than Pope's lack of diplomacy was that he was rash. He was the opposite of McClellan, who moved slowly. The troops of the old regular army were well aware of Pope's habit of acting too hastily. Their nickname for him was "Headquarters-in-the-Saddle."

To fight Lee, General Pope marched his Union Army down the hot dirt roads toward Manassas Junction, the scene of the First Battle of Bull Run. The soldiers were not well disciplined. Often they would yell at their senior officers when they saw them riding by. They would chant, "Hardtack! Hardtack! Hardtack!" This was the way the soldiers let their high-ranking officers know they were hungry. This cry often went up when the wagon trains fell behind and the only thing to eat was the hard, oblong biscuits the men carried in their haversacks.

These were fine people, but in John Pope they had a mediocre, foolhardy leader.

Facing General Pope was Robert E. Lee, one of the great military leaders of all time. Few generals have had a grip on their men such as Lee had on his Army of Northern Virginia. When he rode by on his horse, "Traveller," the Confederate soldiers would take off their hats and call, "Here comes Marse Robert!" or, "Howdy, Uncle Robert!" The Confederates believed in Lee. Even when they were low on rations, or without

shoes on a march, his men followed where Lee led the way. The
gray-clad soldiers realized that General Lee was not only a mas-
ter military leader, but that he was unselfish. He was not for
himself, he was for his men.

Lee was one of the most imaginative generals in the war. Now
that he had located the Union general, John Pope, Lee figured
the way to beat him was to send Stonewall Jackson and the
foot cavalry on a swing to get in Pope's rear.

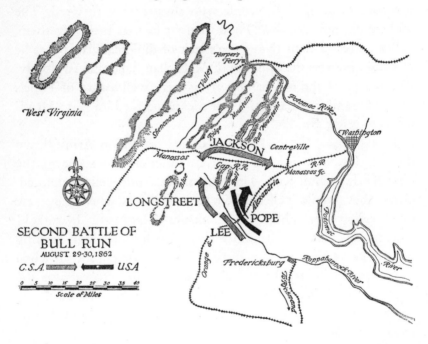

After sending Stonewall Jackson, Lee ordered General Longstreet to follow in Jackson's footsteps. Robert Lee was taking a
chance in splitting his army, but he knew John Pope. Lee felt he
could gamble and win.

Stonewall Jackson led his foot cavalry down the dusty roads
through the August heat, and close behind him came "Old Pete"
Longstreet. When Longstreet had gone a few miles, his men

fell out to the side of the road to rest. General Longstreet had not given the command to halt, so he galloped to the head of the column. He was angry.

"Why have your men stopped?" Longstreet demanded of the colonel of the leading regiment.

"Sir, because that man riding back down the road told us to do so," was the answer. "He said he had orders for us to stop and take a long rest."

"Go get that man!" bellowed Longstreet.

Horsemen galloped after the civilian, who was dressed almost like the Confederate soldiers. They haled him before Longstreet.

"Who gave you authority to halt the column?" snapped the general.

"I have orders from General Longstreet himself," said the man. "He wants this column to stop here."

Longstreet put his hand on his pistol. "I am General Longstreet," he said.

Then the general ordered the man hanged from a tree by the side of the road. Before he died the man said he was a Virginian acting as a spy in the pay of General John Pope.

General Longstreet put his men back on the road and pushed on behind Stonewall Jackson. By this time Jackson was racing through Thoroughfare Gap in the Bull Run Mountains. This put Stonewall behind John Pope's Federal Army. The men in blue were in a trap, and Stonewall tore up the railroad at Manassas Junction while he waited for Lee to spring the jaws of the trap.

John Pope ordered his men to attack the foot cavalry. For a while the battle was even. Then Pope's rashness threw him. Stonewall Jackson's men moved back a few hundred yards to get behind a steep railroad embankment. When John Pope saw this, he was delirious with joy. He thought Stonewall Jackson was retreating and he did not send scouts forward to check.

Pope wrote out and sent a hasty telegram to Washington saying he had won a great battle.

Word now came to Pope that General Longstreet had come up on Stonewall Jackson's right, and that part of Longstreet's men were in hiding. This did not bother Pope. He ignored this information. The foolhardy "Headquarters-in-the-Saddle" Pope now issued orders for his men to *chase* Stonewall Jackson!

The men in blue ran forward and Jackson's soldiers, behind the embankment, mowed them down. Both sides fought bravely in fierce, hand-to-hand combat. General Longstreet's artillery-men had wonderful targets, and his riflemen came out of hiding and fired into the Union ranks. The trap was sprung and many Union men fell. Iron cannon balls plowed into the blue lines and bounced over the countryside like huge rubber balls. Finally, the Federals broke and headed for Washington.

There was great confusion in the Union Army at a stone bridge on the Warrenton Turnpike. Pope, thinking he would have no trouble, had his wagon trains close to the battlefield, and now they jammed the roads. The civilian sutlers turned their wagons around and whipped their horses in a wild dash toward Washington. Union artillery, infantry, wagon trains, cavalry, sutlers' vehicles, and staff officers were caught in a traffic jam on the turnpike. To add to the misery, when night came it began to rain.

On the retreat, the downhearted Yankee army spied General John Pope by the side of the road. "Traitor!" many shouted. They despised the rash leader who had led them into the trap.

The retreat to Washington was disorderly, but, thanks to the Union general, Franz Sigel, it was not a rout like the First Battle of Bull Run. Franz Sigel protected the rear of the Union Army, but Lee captured 7,000 prisoners.

Abe Lincoln now had all he could stand of John Pope. The President replaced him with an amazing choice—he put General

George McClellan back in command. But this cheered the Union soldiers, for they still believed they could win with "Little Mac" at their head.

Among the wounded in the mule-drawn ambulances heading for Washington were two brothers, soldiers of the 8th Illinois Cavalry. A doctor told them they were in bad condition. The elder of the two, Sergeant Kemper, looked at his younger brother. "Let's sing 'The Star-Spangled Banner,'" the sergeant said.

The brothers sang, and when it was finished the sergeant died. When the ambulance reached Washington, the younger brother was dead.

In Company K of the 1st Pennsylvania Infantry was Private "Snap" Rouzer. He was not a great soldier, but the men in his company thought he was funny because he was always in trouble. He was one of those men who amused everyone near him whether he tried to do so or not. On the retreat, Snap got tired and lagged farther and farther behind his company. He saw a pigpen and, as there were no pigs in it, Snap decided to take a short rest. He climbed the wooden bars and lay down.

When he awoke, the road was filled with Confederates. Snap Rouzer lay still. Capture meant death or confinement in a Southern prison camp. After a while the Confederates disappeared and Snap got out of the pen. After a long search he found Company K. The captain was mad at him for being absent.

Snap said he had been on a scout, and he told the captain what he had seen. He gave the direction the Confederates had taken and other details. The captain took Snap to the major. The major took Snap to the colonel. The colonel had him escorted to a general. All listened to Snap Rouzer's story.

When Snap got back to his company he told how glad the officers were to get his wonderful information. Snap said he expected to be promoted to lieutenant. The men laughed and teased him. They were right: Snap Rouzer received no promotion.

After the Second Battle of Bull Run, the road to Washington was wide open, but Lee did not take it, for he and President Jefferson Davis had another idea.

With bands playing "Maryland, My Maryland," General Lee crossed the Potomac and headed for Hagerstown. He hoped the presence of his army would cause great numbers of Marylanders to join the Confederate colors. Lee knew his army was not ready to invade the North, for more than six thousand of his men were barefooted, but Lee believed the risk and suffering would be worth while if Maryland became Southern territory.

The Young Napoleon faced the task of stopping Lee, and he was lucky. Private B. W. Mitchell, of the 27th Indiana Volunteers, saw a piece of paper on the ground. He picked it up and read it. It was an order giving Lee's plans, and the order was rushed at top speed to McClellan. How the paper was lost, and how it came to be in the path of the 27th is still a mystery.

When General McClellan read the secret order, he was delighted. He held up the paper, clicked his heels, and cried excitedly, "If I don't crush Lee now, you may call me whatever you please!"

With the benefit of their secret information, the Union Army marched for General Lee. Shortly, at Antietam Creek, just north of Sharpsburg, Maryland, the Union advance guard appeared on Lee's line of march. Robert E. Lee was amazed. McClellan was not acting like McClellan.

The Southern leader found himself in a tight situation. He needed Stonewall Jackson, but Stonewall was busy at Harper's Ferry taking 11,000 prisoners and 13,000 weapons.

When Lee's messengers galloped to Stonewall Jackson and

reported McClellan's smart move, Stonewall shook his head. "I thought I knew McClellan," he said mournfully.

But George McClellan was slow again. General Jackson led the foot cavalry on another fast march and reported to Lee in time to fight.

McClellan had 70,000 Union troops. Against him, Lee had but 55,000.

One might have expected a crushing Union victory. However, General McClellan did not use all his men, and the Union soldiers who were ordered to fight were not employed as a complete unit.

There were horrible losses on both sides. The Battle of Antietam was even bloodier than Shiloh. Thousands of homes on both sides eventually received the news that a loved one had fallen at Antietam Creek.

There was no real winner. There never is in such a battle. The Confederates marched back to Virginia with very few Marylanders along.

General McClellan was at last relieved from command by the very patient Lincoln. The President told his wife, "I hate to see McClellan go. He and I had grown to understand each other so well."

Chapter 15

LINCOLN TURNS THE WAR
INTO A CRUSADE

PRESIDENT LINCOLN faced hard times. He was more determined than ever to bring the Southern states back into the Union, but the war was becoming unpopular in the North. A group of Northerners tried to stop the fighting and plotted to overthrow the government. These men were called "Copperheads." They pointed to the rising cost of living and the growing lists of dead and wounded. Clement Vallandigham, the leader of the Copperheads, made bitter speeches trying to embarrass the war effort and Lincoln.

Lincoln quieted Vallandigham by having soldiers arrest him, take him under a flag of truce and, against his will, place him on the Southern side. This helped some, but to many thousands in the North it looked as if the Union could not defeat the Southerners. The Confederates had Robert E. Lee, Stonewall Jackson, Jim Longstreet, Jeb Stuart, and other leaders whom the Yankees had been unable to defeat. The Copperheads noted that the Union Army could not even put down the dashing Virginian who operated at night behind the Federal lines, John Mosby. Mosby and his 200 daredevils on horseback, on one midnight raid, even captured a Union general. Chasing Mosby, many Northerners said, was like pursuing a will-o'-the-wisp.

Things looked black for the North, but Lincoln had an idea. In fact, he had had it for a long time. His thought was to free the slaves in the states that were fighting the Union.

Some time back President Lincoln had discussed with General McClellan the possibility of freeing slaves in the Southern states. "Little Mac" assured the President that such action would be a great mistake. McClellan had said his army would not fight if it got the idea that the war was being fought to free the slaves. McClellan gave Lincoln a lot of advice against the proposition. The Secretary of State, William Seward, told the President that *if* he freed the slaves he must pick a time when a Northern army was victorious, otherwise people would think it a gesture of despair. Lincoln listened, but he kept the proclamation to free the slaves in his pocket while he thought it over.

When Lee led his army back to Virginia after the Battle of Antietam, President Lincoln decided the time had arrived. The Federals had not won a victory, yet Lee had to go back for men and supplies. Lincoln now made his greatest decision. He called a meeting of his cabinet and said that on January 1, 1863, all slaves in the *South* would be free.

"How," people asked, "can he free slaves in enemy territory?"

Newspaper writers and cartoonists made fun of the Emancipation Proclamation, as this act of Lincoln was called. The New York *World* said Abe Lincoln was a fanatic, and the London *Times* called him names. Some said the slaves would revolt and murder their former masters. A few Union soldiers appeared in the Southern lines saying they would fight no more, because they had not enlisted to free Negroes.

But the great majority of the Federal soldiers quickly saw that the freeing of the slaves would hurt the South. The three to four million slaves in the Confederacy represented power and wealth to their owners, and the soldiers rightly believed that thousands of slaves would come to the Union Army at their first chance. This was true, although many other thousands remained on the plantations to help their former owners.

The slaves themselves were happy, although many were confused because they did not know what to expect now that "Massa Linkum" had set them free.

Leaders of nations in Europe saw at once that they could not afford to fight on the Southern side, as President Jeff Davis had hoped. No European country desired to fight against a people who had announced such a high purpose.

The touchy border states were not upset by Lincoln's proclamation, for he did not free their slaves. That would come later.

The Union soldiers in the front lines were delighted with Lincoln's action. They now had an even higher cause for which to fight. Abraham Lincoln had truly turned the war into a crusade.

Chapter 16

FREDERICKSBURG—SLAUGHTER ON THE RAPPAHANNOCK

W ITH McClellan gone, Lincoln looked over his senior generals. He chose Ambrose E. Burnside to command the army. He could hardly have made a poorer choice.

General Burnside's plan to defeat Lee was to cross the Rappahannock River at Fredericksburg and attack head on. Lincoln checked the plan and did not like it, but he gave in, telling Burnside he must move fast if he were to succeed.

The plan of attack hinged on building three pontoon bridges across the Rappahannock and rushing the men across. Burnside marched his army to the river, but there was an eight-day delay while the pontoon boats, which were to support the bridge, were hauled from Harper's Ferry to Fredericksburg. During this time General Lee's scouts gave him accurate information on the Federal Army.

Lee placed a huge army in trenches on Marye's Heights above the colonial town of Fredericksburg and along the plain to the east. He made the place into a military strong point six miles long.

When the Union engineer soldiers started to build their bridges over the river, General William Barksdale's Mississippi sharpshooters began to fire from Fredericksburg. The sharpshooters knocked so many bridgebuilders into the water that one Union private called the Rappahannock "the river of death." General Barksdale sent a message to Lee saying that if Lee wanted a "bridge of dead Yankees" he had one for him.

The Union engineers made nine attempts to get bridges across the river, but the fire of the Mississippians made it an impossible task. So the Union artillery pounded the town and the Federal troops grabbed the pontoon boats and rowed across the river.

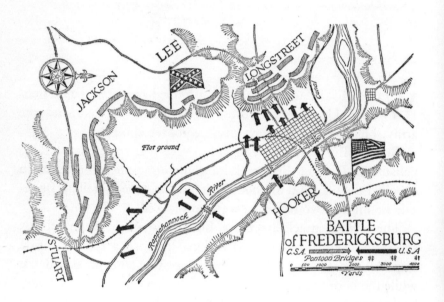

When the 7th Michigan Regiment went across, Bob Hendershot, a drummer boy twelve years old, jumped into a boat. An officer ordered him ashore. Bob jumped out of the boat, helped shove it into the water, but held onto the stern and was carried across. Here a Confederate shell ruined his drum. He picked up a musket and rounded up a wounded enemy soldier. Bob got the man back to the other side of the Rappahannock and, while taking him to the rear, ran into General Burnside. Burnside said,

"Boy, I like your courage. You keep it up and you'll be in my place."

One hundred and forty-seven cannons fired cannon balls into the village of Fredericksburg. Smoke and flames from the buildings made it a ghastly scene. When the bridges were finally built, General William Franklin marched his men across with a band playing at the head of the column and flags flying. It was an unbelievable entry into an attack.

Stonewall Jackson had the blond John Pelham on the right of the battle line with Jeb Stuart. Young Pelham's cannons mowed the Federal troops down as they charged from the river across the plain. Two of Pelham's cannons were so far out in front of the Confederate infantry that they were almost captured.

Up on Marye's Heights, behind a stone wall, the Confederates blasted the approaching blue ranks. In spite of the pointblank rifle and cannon fire, the Federals kept coming back. *Fourteen* desperate, piecemeal, and unsupported attacks were made by the Union troops against the hill. Each assault was straight ahead with little chance of succeeding. General Burnside did not search for a "soft spot" that he could take first, or try to maneuver.

Before the battle, when the Yankee soldiers heard of the plan of attack, they knew they had little chance. Many wrote letters home, realizing the messages they were sending might be the last they would ever despatch to their families.

The citizens of Fredericksburg also took a terrible beating. Numbers of them left the town before the battle started, but many others would not desert their homes. The town caught on fire.

All except one brigade of the Federals were driven back across the river as night fell. At daybreak, the general of the brigade asked for volunteers to take a message across the river to get help. One brave private volunteered to go. The general wrote out the message while the private's friends told him good-by. It looked to be certain death for the soldier, as the enemy fired at anyone who showed his head. The private started for the bridge at a dead run. Enemy rifles cracked and bullets tore up the ground where the soldier ran. Suddenly he fell. Up went a taunting cry from the Rebels: "Send another one!" The soldier's friends were consoling themselves about his death when suddenly he jumped up and streaked for the river. He had fooled the Confederates, and lived to deliver his message, which helped part of his brigade to get back.

The Union General Burnside planned another set of attacks in the same place, to be executed in the same manner. However, his senior officers talked him out of the idea.

The people of Fredericksburg now started the tremendous task of burying the dead. Marye's Hill and the meadows along the river were dotted with soldiers in blue who would never move again—9,000 fell on Marye's Heights alone. Lee's Army of Northern Virginia had 5,300 dead.

When General Burnside pulled his army back, Stonewall Jackson suggested to Lee that the Confederates pull off their clothes, cross the river, and attack. Lee did not approve.

The senior generals in the Union Army were disturbed by Burnside's horrible failure, especially a handsome general named Hooker. President Lincoln finally accepted Burnside's resignation as commanding general and began a search for a man who could lead. He thought of Joseph Hooker. Perhaps he was a winner. His nickname was "Fighting Joe."

On the last day of 1862 the Union Army near Murfreesboro, in central Tennessee, five hundred miles from Fredericksburg, was under pressure from Washington to attack. The Federals carried out their orders and marched against the Confederates at Stones River. Although it was not a decisive battle, the men in gray withdrew.

At Stones River there was a Union general, a splendid husky fellow, who had fuzzy whiskers. His name was George H. Thomas. His soldiers liked him because he was stout-hearted and kind. They had many nicknames for General Thomas: "Uncle George," "Pap," and "Old Pap." Someday he would become one of the greatest Union generals.

Chapter 17

VICKSBURG

THE most important Confederate stronghold on the Mississippi River was the fortified city of Vicksburg. Only Richmond, the capital of the Confederacy, meant more to the Southerners. As long as the South had Vicksburg, cattle and other supplies from the great plains of Texas could be transported to the Confederate armies, and the Union could not use the whole length of the river. At the time of the attack on Vicksburg the South had already lost New Orleans, Memphis, and Baton Rouge.

Vicksburg, high on the bluffs on the east bank of the Mississippi, was guarded by the marshy and gloomy Yazoo River on the north, by stinking swamps to the south, and by more than thirty thousand soldiers in and near the city. A former United States Army officer, Lieutenant General John C. Pemberton, of the Confederacy, was in command. Pemberton had fortified Vicksburg by placing powerful cannons on the bluffs near the river, and by building a long system of trenches.

Two stanch Union commanders, General U. S. Grant and Commodore David Porter, worked at the task of taking the city.

Commodore Porter, the son of a famous naval officer, had been a midshipman as a boy and had fought in the Mexican War.

He was a cocky and experienced sea dog who believed in his ships and in the men who manned them. But things on the Mississippi were not easy for him. About a year before Grant tackled the city, the Confederates all but wrecked Porter's fleet with the powerful ram, the *Arkansas*. The *Ark* had three inches of railroad iron on her sides and a sharp prow, but finally the *Ark's* engines failed and the Confederates blew her up so that Porter's fleet would not get her.

General Grant had *his* troubles. "Old Brains" Halleck, far away in Washington, was trying to tell Grant what to do by telegraph. In addition, many of Grant's men were sick from malaria. Then, in August, the Confederate cavalryman, Earl Van Dorn, captured two million dollars' worth of supplies at Holly Springs, Mississippi. The Confederate horseman took all the supplies his wagons could carry and put the rest to the torch. It was an unhappy time for General Grant.

Life was harsh also in the city of Vicksburg. The Southerners in the town were forced to dig caves in the clay banks of the city to protect their families from the shells of Porter's gunboats. Food and medicines were getting scarce. Provisions for the city became even harder to get when Colonel Ben Grierson took 1,700 cavalrymen and raided the country from Tennessee to southern Louisiana.

Grant tried plan after plan to capture the city. Even the rainy weather seemed to favor the Confederates. Finally, Grant decided that if Commodore Porter could transport the army down the river, he could attack Vicksburg from the east.

The general ordered his men to dig a canal out of reach of the Confederates' cannons. The idea was to make the river change its course. If water would go through the canal, Grant would have Porter carry the army safely down the river. Once below Vicksburg, the general would put his men ashore on the east bank and march up toward the city.

When Lincoln heard about the idea of the canal he liked it. He had been on the great river as a boy and knew that it often changed its course.

Cutting the canal through the cypress swamps was the toughest kind of work. Thousands of men labored. Tree trunks had to be cut off under water. Men had a difficult time finding dry land on which to pitch a tent. Grant helped by bringing in two dredges.

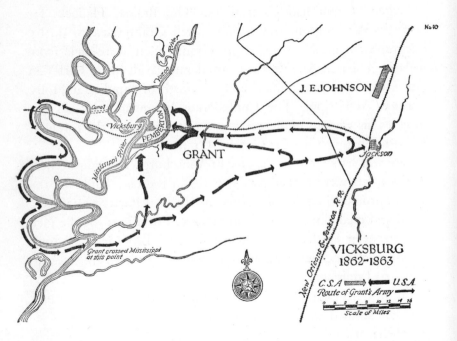

General Pemberton was equal to this move. He sent a battery of artillery against the dredges and sharpshooters against the men sawing wood, but Grant had his infantrymen move into the swamps as protection for the workers. When the canal was finally dug, the river fell and water would not enter it.

But Grant did not give up. He tried still another plan. He asked Porter to run his gunboats past the city. Grant said he would march his men down the west bank and join Porter far downstream.

Commodore Porter was agreeable. He called for volunteers to man his ships, men who were not afraid, and he got them. Soldiers came who had been deck hands, engineers, pilots, and ship captains. Porter placed bales of cotton and sacks of grain at vital spots in the ships so the Confederate cannon balls would not kill his men and put his vessels out of action.

One dark night Porter's fleet got up steam. "Full speed ahead!" was the order. Downstream swept the gunboats. But the Confederates were alert. They lit huge piles of wood and the night became "day." Porter, on his flagship, the fortified steamboat *Blackhawk*, said the scene was "magnificent but terrifying."

The cannons on the bluffs roared. Cannon balls thudded into the Yankee ships and skipped about the water. But the Confederate gunners, who were under fire from guns on the ships, did not have much success. Although every vessel was hit, only one ship was sunk.

The general took his soldiers on a winding march south, well away from the fire of the Confederate cannons. With him was his thirteen-year-old son, Fred, who often held the general's horse when the general needed a horse-holder. Far below Vicksburg, Commodore Porter ferried Grant's men across the river.

Grant was now ready to march against the city, but he had no supply line from the Northern states, no route over which food could reach him. Many, including his best general, William Tecumseh Sherman, thought Grant's plan was no good. Sherman was worried not only about feeding so large an army, but he pointed out that the Confederate General Joe Johnston was forty miles east of Vicksburg with an army.

So Grant set out to defeat Johnston. The march was not easy. It was hot, and the roads in the canebrakes were swampy. Durell's Battery, an independent artillery battery from Pennsylvania, crossed a bayou. There was a rickety log bridge and that was all. It looked unsafe for the heavy ammunition caisson, so Captain Durell ordered the first two pair of horses to be unhitched and led across. Joseph Lear, the driver, started across slowly with only two horses pulling the heavy cart. Suddenly the bridge gave way, and Lear and the horses were thrown into the water. The horses thrashed about, struggling to free themselves from their heavy harness. Men in a canoe rescued Lear but the horses could not be saved. Captain Durell drew his pistol. He took aim and shot the two horses, and the battery moved on, unable to recover the ammunition.

After a successful fight against Johnston, General Grant lay siege to Vicksburg, and the suffering of the people in the city increased. Their food supplies became lower and lower. They had a biscuit and a little bacon a day. When that was gone, they ate horses, dogs, cats, and rats. Mule soup was hard to drink. The Vicksburg newspaper was printed on wallpaper. The sick had no medicine.

Grant sent foraging details out over the country to bring in meat, chicken, and molasses for his army. Of course, this was very hard on the people of Mississippi.

The Union leader and his men were much better off than the people in the city, except that measles, smallpox, and other diseases broke out in the Federal forces. Captain Crozer, of Iowa, wrote, "... Our men burnt several very fine Houses, the furniture, 2 Pianos, 5 large Cotton Gins, and a sawmill combined with a pile of Cotton. It looks like a pity to destroy everything ... but we will devastate the country and teach them a lesson they won't soon forget."

Thousands of Negroes came to Grant to be fed. To make them earn their food, he employed many as teamsters and cooks. For the rest he established a "Freedmen's Bureau." The Negroes cut wood for the steamers and picked cotton on abandoned plantations. Grant arranged for any nearby plantation owners who desired to hire the "Freedmen" to be able to do so.

The hot summer dragged on. The Confederates in the city would not surrender. They pinned their faith on General Johnston's being able to come to their rescue. At night the privates of the two armies often met between the lines to trade coffee and to talk.

To hasten the end, Grant ordered a series of attacks on the breastworks. There were many instances of courage and heroism on both sides. In one attack, sixty Union soldiers reached part of the Confederate works. The Union men planted two colors on the parapets of the trenches and prepared to defend their flags.

Captain Bradley, commanding the Texas legion, gathered his

men for a counterattack. Colonel Pettus, of Alabama, grabbed his musket and went along with the Texans. There was vicious hand-to-hand fighting before the Union men retired and the Texans captured the United States colors.

General Pemberton wrote to General Grant:

Sir,

Two days have passed since your dead and wounded have been left lying in our front. . . . I have the honor to propose the fighting stop for 2½ hours so you can remove your dead. . . .

Very respectfully, your obedient servant,
J. C. Pemberton
Lieutenant General Commanding

In the two and a half hours the Union side brought in 3,000 dead and wounded.

There was no hope for the Confederates; no one could come to their aid. Even their lowest rations gave out. After consulting with his generals, Pemberton surrendered his brave army after forty-seven days of siege. The date was July 4, 1863.

Grant would not allow his men to cheer when the Confederates marched out. He ordered rations given to the Southerners and medicines for their sick. Then he paroled Pemberton's army. That is, he allowed any man to go home who would sign under oath that he would not fight any more. Several hundred refused to sign and Grant sent them to Northern prison camps.

General Halleck was not pleased that Grant would free more than thirty-one thousand Confederates on parole. Grant said that he was certain these men had had enough war, that they would keep their pledge, and, besides, the cost of sending such a number to prison camps in the North was too great.

Sam Grant now proceeded to clear his enemy out of Jackson, Mississippi. The Iowan Captain Crozer wrote while on the march, ". . . You would be surprised to see the whites & Blacks that are following us, there is fifty teams detailed to carry their effects. Most of them are going North to live...."

Grant sent a brigade to Natchez, on the Mississippi, where they captured 5,000 head of Texas beef cattle and ammunition on the way to Lee.

It was a successful campaign from the Union point of view, but a hard one. General Grant had wrecked General Pemberton's army and captured Vicksburg, which opened the Mississippi and split the Confederacy in two. The control of the river was important. Grant's strategy and courage to keep on when things looked black put new life into the people of the North.

Chapter 18

RAILROAD RAIDERS—BATTLE
AT CHANCELLORSVILLE

JIM ANDREWS, spy for the Union, stood in the center of the tent and waited. What would the general say? Major General Ormsby Mitchell glared at the map before him on the rickety camp table. Outside, a sentry paced back and forth to keep everyone away from the secret conference between the general and the spy.

If what this spy says is true, thought the general, this is our chance to wreck the Western and Atlantic Railroad. If his plan works, the Rebels in Chattanooga soon will be hurting for supplies. Only trouble is it might mean death for the men who go on the raid.

As if reading the general's thoughts, the spy pointed out, "Sir, I've been behind their lines more than two hundred miles. Been all the way to Atlanta. No one paid any attention to me. Give me two dozen volunteers, General, men who know something about a railroad, and you won't regret it."

On a dark night a week later twenty-four volunteers left General Mitchell's lines north of Chattanooga in small groups and drifted south. The Raiders were disguised as Southern civilians. This in itself was dangerous, for a soldier caught out of uniform in enemy country can expect to be hanged.

The Raiders told people who asked that they were on their way to join the Confederate Army. The small groups had little trouble getting south, and in Marietta they assembled in a hotel room where Jim Andrews gave them their mission. "Our job," he said, "is to capture a Rebel train known as The General and run it north. We'll stop every so often and tear up the tracks. We'll cut telegraph wires and burn bridges." The men gasped. It looked like suicide. Jim gave each man a chance to withdraw, but none did.

"That's a single-track railroad," one Raider said. "Suppose we meet oncoming trains? What do we do?"

"I got a timetable," Jim said. "We won't meet many and, besides, I have a plan that'll get us through."

It was raining when the Raiders boarded The General northbound, at Marietta, Georgia. Each Raider took his seat and acted as if he were a regular passenger. At the town of Big Shanty the train wheezed to a stop and the passengers went into the station for breakfast. Even the conductor and engineer left the train. The Raiders held their breath. This was their chance. But across the tracks was a Confederate camp full of soldiers. A sentry stood close by the engine.

The soldiers in the camp paid little attention to the train because they were interested in keeping out of the rain. The sentry under the eave of the station was a sleepy fellow, not alert.

The Raiders uncoupled part of the train and jumped aboard. A Raider in the cab yanked the throttle back and the train chugged out of the station. Big Shanty was soon in an uproar as The General pulled away. A few shots were fired at the train but no one was hit.

As soon as they could, the Raiders stopped to cut the telegraph wires so word of their theft could not flash ahead. They worked feverishly to damage the track, but out of Big Shanty rolled two Confederates on a handcar. The Raiders hopped aboard their stolen train and sped northward.

The General whistled for the crossings. Black smoke poured out of the funnel-shaped stack as the men piled the firebox full of wood. The train tore around curves at top speed. Up the track a southbound train waited for The General. Jim Andrews hopped down from the cab and shouted, "Back your train up to the siding! Right away! Let us through. We have powder for General Beauregard."

Andrew's trick worked, and the stolen train rumbled ahead as fast as it could go. Every time the Raiders passed a station it was necessary to stop so they could cut the telegraph wires. There was little chance to damage the tracks because the Southerners were close behind, and the rain prevented the Northerners from setting the bridges on fire.

Wood for The General began to get low. The Raiders tore up the planks of the box car that was riding behind the engine, and fed them into the fire box. Behind them, and gaining, roared the Confederate train, The Texas.

At the end of ninety miles the stolen train chuffed to a stop. It was out of wood. The Raiders jumped and ran for their lives, but the Confederates soon rounded them up.

To try to make the young Raider Joseph Parrott tell the details about the plot, a Confederate lieutenant whipped him almost to death with a rawhide whip, but Parrott would not talk. The Raiders were court-martialed. Jim Andrews and seven of his men were hanged. The rest were thrown into prison, but escaped and beat their way north.

One year later six of the brave Raiders stood in Secretary of War Stanton's office, where Abraham Lincoln shook their hands. "Congress has voted the men who went on the raid the first

Medals of Honor," he said. The President thanked every Raider present, and Mr. Stanton gave each man one hundred dollars.

It was when Lincoln realized that the Army of the Potomac had lost confidence in its leader that he replaced General Burnside with General Hooker.

There had been many inspiring acts of bravery in the Union Army at the terrible Battle of Fredericksburg, but in spite of this the morale of the army was low. New recruits arrived to take the places of the men who had been killed and wounded, but many soldiers deserted.

Joseph Hooker, a West Point graduate, was talkative but full of energy. He had fought in Mexico before the Civil War and had a dashing nickname. The soldiers called him "Fighting Joe." He looked like a soldier.

Fighting Joe's sharp tongue was a worry to Abe Lincoln. The President told this handsome general that the habit of criticism which Hooker had helped instill in the army might now turn against him. The President meant that because Hooker had not been loyal to people over him the officers might not be loyal to Hooker. Lincoln also told the general he *must* win.

First Hooker worked to improve his army. He was the first to get the idea of having each of his corps (about fifteen thousand men) wear a separate badge on their caps. The insignia were of different designs; the colors were red, white, and blue. In the beginning the men made their own badges. They liked them, for it gave each man a sense of belonging. Hooker also improved the furlough system so that every soldier had a chance to go home and visit his loved ones. The spirit of the army began to strengthen. The Union soldiers believed they could win under Fighting Joe.

Hooker showed his army to the President in a grand review. Mr. and Mrs. Lincoln arrived in a carriage, escorted by a troop

of cavalry. The equipment of the horsemen jingled as they trotted past the President's vehicle. Young Tad Lincoln rode a pony
close by. A boy dressed in a trooper's uniform acted as Tad's
orderly.

One hundred and thirty-four thousand men paraded. They
showed "Father Abraham," as the soldiers called him, they were
ready to crush Lee, who had only 60,000.

Fighting Joe Hooker explained his plan to Lincoln. It looked
easy. He would keep Lee busy at Fredericksburg. At the same
time, the main part of the Union Army would swing twenty-five
miles upstream on a secret march. Fighting Joe would send this
part of his army across the Rappahannock River to cut in behind
the Confederates. It was a splendid idea and the President liked
it.

But Hooker stopped his men soon after they crossed the river,
near a small place called Chancellorsville. Fighting Joe had lost
his nerve. The woods were thick and his cavalrymen failed to
bring him information about the enemy. Things did not look so
simple as they had when he explained the plan to President
Lincoln.

The two armies were in a section of Virginia known as the
Wilderness. It was a country of stunted, scrubby trees and
heavy thickets. In some places the ground was swampy, in
others the holly trees grew close together. There were thickets
of bushy firs and cedars tangled in webs of vines and briars.

As rugged as the country was, Jeb Stuart's cavalry scouts kept
Lee informed of Hooker's right-end swing. Lee knew exactly
what Hooker planned to do and he called for Stonewall Jackson.
Lee and Jackson sat on two ration boxes before a campfire and
planned the battle.

"Let me take my men and go around," Stonewall said. "I can
come in on Hooker's right flank. I'll surprise him."

"How many of your men will you take?" asked Lee.

"All of 'em."

Lee thought awhile, then approved Stonewall's plan.

On his daring march through the back country to surprise the Federals, Stonewall's rear guard was attacked.

"Push on," said Stonewall. "Keep going. Our main job's ahead. Press on!"

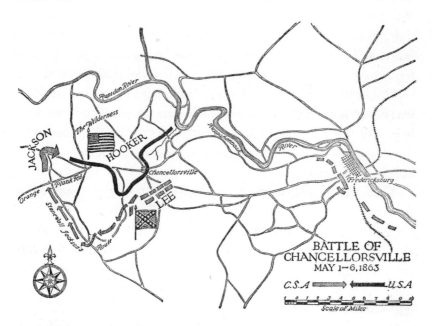

Stonewall Jackson had a great sense of mission—he was determined to carry out his main job. When his men burst through the woods screaming the Rebel yell, there was wild confusion in Hooker's right wing. Pack mules carrying Union ammunition stampeded through Union soldiers on the Orange Plank Road.

Confederate bullets tore into the surprised Union soldiers. The Union soldiers ran for the river. General Oliver Howard, of the State of Maine, his one arm holding the reins of his horse and the stump of his other holding the Stars and Stripes, tried to stop the horde of frightened Union soldiers without success.

Near dusk Stonewall Jackson rode out to the front of his army to scout the enemy. When he galloped back along the Orange Plank Road in the darkness, shots rang out. Confederate pickets, men guarding the lines, had hit Stonewall Jackson.

Jackson's left arm was badly wounded. Blood poured into his gauntlets. His men carried him tenderly to the rear on a litter. Muskets roared in the darkness and one of the litter-bearers was shot. Young Sandie Pendleton galloped for the surgeon. To save Stonewall, the doctor amputated the general's arm. Lee was horror-stricken that his best general was seriously wounded.

The battle in the tangled woods raged for four more days. It was horrible in the thickets at night when the wounded called for help and for water. Red flashes cut through the darkness as infantrymen fired their rifles. Cannons belched grapeshot and canister at close range.

Then the woods caught fire. The screams of the wounded, as the fire crept toward them, were beyond description.

In the middle of the battle Fighting Joe Hooker stood on the porch of a house, leaning against a pillar. A cannon ball tore into the pillar and rubble crashed into Hooker, knocking him senseless. He was in a daze for the rest of the battle. The vain and dashing Joe Hooker was hardly in command of his army.

Fighting Joe, outgeneraled and outfought, ordered the remainder of his huge army back across the river. He had lost 17,000 men and had left Lee in command of the Wilderness. The stench of the place was awful.

Lee captured 5,000 Yankees, many guns, and much ammunition. It was a victory for the South, but there was little rejoicing on the Confederate side, for they had lost 13,000 men and the great Stonewall Jackson was dying.

The doctors worked to save Stonewall, but his life was ebbing away. He realized he was dying. He asked what day it was.

"Sunday," was the answer. Stonewall replied, "I always wanted to die on Sunday."

Now his mind became hazy. Once more he thought he was at the head of his army. "Tell A. P. Hill to push them back. Push the attack!" Then Jackson spoke his last words, "Let us cross the river and rest under the shade of the trees."

Jackson's closest friends buried him at Lexington, Virginia. Lee could not go to the funeral, because the Army of the Potomac was across the Rappahannock.

The Battle of Chancellorsville stamped Robert E. Lee as one of the leading generals of all time, but the winning team of Lee and Jackson had been wrecked. The loss was a great one for Lee, for he never found anyone to take Stonewall's place.

Abraham Lincoln was heartbroken when he heard the news of the Union defeat. "What will the country say!" he exclaimed. "What will the country say!"

The spirit of criticism that Hooker had helped instill in the Union Army now rose against him. The officers asked Lincoln for a new general in command and, in desperation, he selected yet another officer, General Meade.

Chapter 19

THE BATTLE OF GETTYSBURG

THE Confederates now decided to let the Northern people have a taste of war at home.

President Jeff Davis and Robert E. Lee believed if they were successful in the enemy's country, the "Copperheads," or anti-war party, would gain ground and the Yankees might stop fighting. With the victories at Fredericksburg and Chancellorsville to encourage them, the Confederates crossed the Potomac and struck for the farm country in Pennsylvania.

General Lee issued orders that his men would not apply the torch. They were on their best behavior, but in spite of this the Pennsylvania farmers did not welcome the Southerners.

On the march north a Confederate scout reported to General Jeb Stuart. The scout told of a Union wagon train of one hundred and fifty wagons that could be captured. Stuart liked daring expeditions. Once more he ordered his cavalry to ride around the Union Army. He could see his men capturing the train and bringing needed supplies to General Lee. But Stuart's decision to raid was a mistake, for cavalry were the "eyes and ears" of a Civil War army, and without Jeb Stuart to send reports on what the Yankees were doing, Lee's huge army marching into enemy country was deaf and blind.

With Lee rode the famous Confederate fighter, General James Longstreet. "Old Pete" commanded almost one third of Lee's army. Old Pete was a bulky, five-foot-ten man who wore a bushy beard. He had been a major in the old army. The soldiers ran up the column to get a look at him when they heard that the famous Old Pete Longstreet was along. The men knew that Longstreet and Lee were the best of friends. They thought with such leaders the Confederate side could not lose.

It was at this time that Lincoln put George Meade at the head of the large Union Army. It was a difficult time to take charge. Meade, a quiet, serious West Pointer, was anxious for high command. He believed in himself and felt competent to lead the 90,000 men under him. The mission, given General Meade by Abraham Lincoln himself, was to defeat Lee's army. The President had decided that the way to win was to conquer the Confederate soldiers. He said that just capturing Richmond would not do it, and he was right.

The two armies met near the quiet town of Gettysburg. The date was July 1, 1863.

Among the first Union troops to arrive were the soldiers of the famous "Iron Brigade," men who wore black hats. Their bands were playing and the soldiers sang. It looked like a gay time. Old John Burns, of Gettysburg, who had had seventy birthdays, grabbed his musket and fell in ranks. The hard fighters of the Iron Brigade teased the old fellow with the swallow-tailed coat. But when they saw that he was in earnest, they stopped laughing. John Burns said, "Which way are the Rebels? I know how to fight. I've fit before."

The first Confederates to march on the scene were commanded by the odd-looking Lieutenant General Dick Ewell. He had been wounded at the Second Battle of Bull Run and had lost a leg. While Dick Ewell was looking over the rolling country-side, a major galloped up with a message from General Lee. Lee wanted Ewell to take Cemetery Hill—"*if possible.*"

Shortly thereafter a well-aimed Minié ball whizzed through the air and smashed into General Ewell's wooden leg. There was no physical pain, but the experience was a shock. Ewell decided that it was *not possible* to put his men on Cemetery Hill.

The Confederates took the town and a ridge to the west, but they failed to seize the key to the battlefield, Cemetery Hill, at the north end of Cemetery Ridge.

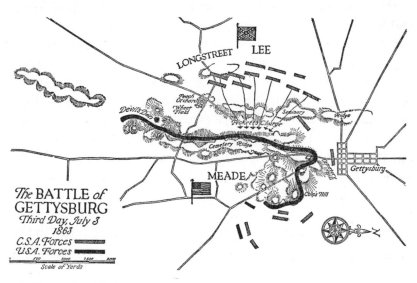

The BATTLE of
GETTYSBURG
*Third Day, July 3
1863*
C.S.A. Forces
U.S.A. Forces
Scale of Yards

When the Union commanding general, George Meade, arrived early on the morning of the second day, he ordered his men to seize the important positions, Cemetery Hill and Culp's Hill. The Yankees set to work at once to make these positions strong.

General Lee wanted to attack early on the second day, but his army was not ready, and Jim Longstreet, his right-hand man, asked bluntly, "Why not fight a defensive battle?" Lee felt that an attack could win, and in his gentle manner he insisted that Longstreet carry out his orders.

General Meade was having his troubles, too. One of his generals, Dan Sickles, who was better at politics than at war, decided he would improve on General Meade's plan without telling Meade. Sickles marched his brigade off Cemetery Ridge and advanced toward the Confederates. When Sickles' men neared a peach orchard, 160 of General Longstreet's cannons blasted them. Confederate sharpshooters hidden in the rocks and crevices of the Devil's Den picked Sickles' soldiers up on the front sights of their muskets, and many men in blue fell to the ground. General Sickles had led his men into a trap.

The Reverend John Bloodgood, who was with Sickles, serving as a sergeant in Company "I," 141st Pennsylvania Volunteers, wrote that above the noise of battle came the orders: "Charge! Forward, guide center, charge!" but Sickles' men could do little to help themselves. A color-bearer of the 141st went down. Colonel Madill, the regimental commander, seized the flag to rally his men. General Sickles himself was badly wounded in the leg and had to be carried to the rear on a litter.

Men from Georgia were mowing down more and more of Sickles' soldiers. The 1st Minnesota Regiment, numbering only 260, was ordered to make a bayonet charge to plug a gap in the lines and to help Sickles' brigade. The Minnesotans carried out their daring charge but lost 215 men.

On the Confederate side, General Longstreet was sulking. He had purposely been slow in arranging the attack Lee had ordered. Longstreet reminded Lee that Jeb Stuart and the cavalry were off on a raid, that there was no real information about the enemy, and that Confederates under General Pickett had not yet come up. Lee was polite but firm. He wanted an attack and as fast as possible.

Old Pete Longstreet walked about with a worried expression

on his face, his eyes on the ground. He told the fighting Texan, General Hood, "General Lee is a little nervous. He wants me to attack, but I don't wish to do so without General Pickett. I never go into battle with one boot off."

Pickett's men were slow arriving, and Longstreet's attacks across the Devil's Den and other places were piecemeal, like Hooker's attacks at Fredericksburg. As a result, many Confederates died.

Sergeant Lamb, carrying the Confederate Stars and Bars, marched in the attack. His comrades thought his flag was drawing fire. They yelled, "Lower the colors! Down with the flag!" But Sergeant Lamb cried, "This flag never goes down till I am down." Despite such spirit and confidence, the Confederate attacks on the second day of the fierce battle were unsuccessful.

On this same day, General Meade ordered his engineer officer, General G. K. Warren, to look over the battlefield—particularly at General Sickles' position, which Meade thought was on Cemetery Ridge, *not* a mile in front. General Warren saw that one of the most important places on the battlefield was the hill, Little Round Top, and that it was unoccupied.

Warren ordered troops there as fast as possible. Men from Maine, New York, Pennsylvania, and Michigan arrived on Little Round Top just as the Confederates dashed up. Vicious hand-to-hand fighting resulted. In quick succession the 19th Indiana Regiment had four color-bearers killed, but the Union soldiers held on to Little Round Top. This smart decision by General Warren was of vital importance to the Union.

The Confederate sharpshooters in the Devil's Den were particularly effective just before the sun went down. Hidden in the jumbled rock pile, the sharpshooters, with the sun at their backs, could pick off troops on Cemetery Ridge with ease. A Union commander sent a patrol to kill the sharpshooters, but it was defeated. The patrol leader reported when he returned to the Union lines, "The dead in the Devil's Den are thicker than autumn leaves."

That night, when Sickles' men got back, officers tried to straighten out the lines and to get the men into companies again. In the 141st Pennsylvania Volunteers an officer called the names of the companies to check how many men were left. When he called, "Company K," one man answered. "I am Company K," he said.

General Meade was very angry at General Sickles, for he had used twenty brigades to get Sickles' men back on Cemetery Ridge.

It had been a blistering July day. In the dusk, some of the men on both sides were able to get cool water at Spangler's Spring. Others were drinking water out of mud puddles and were thankful. The calls of the wounded, begging for water, were pitiful. Stretcher-bearers and surgeons worked overtime.

That night Stuart's cavalry came back from their raid. They had scant information about the Federals, although they had many trophies. They were too exhausted to be of great use. Old Pete Longstreet was furious.

Longstreet came to Lee on the morning of the third day and said, "Sir, my scouts were out all night and have brought me information. I believe I can make General Meade attack us." But Lee again overruled him. The great Confederate leader knew the previous attacks had not been coordinated. There had been no teamwork. He wanted to take Cemetery Ridge, and before more Federals arrived.

General Longstreet pointed out that men advancing across the mile of meadowlike ground from the Confederate lines would come under cannon fire from Little Round Top. One member of Lee's staff thought the Union artillery could be silenced.

In the Confederate plan, General Pickett was given the job of smashing the Yankee center. First, there would be a two-hour artillery cannonade to help him. Confederate chaplains came to the front of Pickett's brigades. The men knelt, bareheaded, while the chaplains prayed. "It is in His hands," said the Confederate general, Lewis Armistead. It was a nervous time for Pickett's men.

At three o'clock the men from Virginia, Alabama, North Carolina, Mississippi, and Tennessee formed two long lines. General Pickett and other leaders rode their horses along the ranks checking the men for the last time. Pickett gave the word, and the mile-long formation marched forward. The drummer boys were tapping their drums. The colors were flying. Fifteen thousand Confederates were marching into the face of 159 cannons and thousands of experienced Union soldiers who were in trenches and behind stone walls.

Union cannon on Little Round Top blasted huge gaps in the butternut-gray ranks. The Confederates swept on. Horses carrying leaders went down. Other horses, their riders in the dirt, dashed frantically about the battlefield trying to escape the crash of the shells. The cannons thundered. The very ground shook.

On Cemetery Ridge, Union riflemen waited nervously for the command to fire. Each soldier in blue realized his responsibility. When the Confederates were in canister range, the Union cannoneers slammed that weapon into the field pieces. The infantrymen in blue now heard the command, *"Ready! Aim! Fire!"*

The screams of the wounded mingled with the blood-tingling Rebel yell as the Confederates charged. The smoke from the black powder and the dust on the ridge added to the confusion. Seventy thousand men grappled at close quarters.

After twenty minutes, Pickett saw that his soldiers could not remain on the ridge and he ordered a retreat. Four Confederate generals, Lewis Armistead, Dick Garnett, James Kemper, and

William Barksdale, lay dead near a grove of trees at the center of the ridge. Armistead died with his hand on a Union cannon. Other fine Southern leaders were killed; many wounded.

Back limped the Confederates from "Pickett's Charge." Some wounded men crawled back, others were carried, and still others used their rifles as crutches. General Lee was heartbroken when he saw the results of the charge. General Pickett lived, but he now had no brigade. Dead men, Confederate and Union, lay everywhere, their sightless eyes staring at the sky.

Lee tried to get ready for a counterattack by Meade, but it did not come. Nor did Meade follow up and try to smash Lee's army when Lee marched his men back to Virginia. General Meade did not move to gain the full fruits of his victory.

In the late afternoon of July 4, news was passed through the Union positions: *Vicksburg had surrendered to Grant.* The soldiers cheered and cheered.

A Union band appeared on Cemetery Ridge and played "Yankee Doodle," "Hail to the Chief," and "The Star-Spangled Banner," but thousands, lying in the Union battle line and on the ground just in front of the ridge, would never hear.

The end of the war now seemed in sight to the men in blue. But not to the Southerners. They had lost a great battle, but their fighting spirit had not been defeated. They would fight on.

Lee felt crushed as he rode toward Virginia, but he was never too low in mind to see the troubles of those beneath him. Beside the road he saw a wounded prisoner of war. The prisoner recognized General Lee and shouted, "Hurrah for the Union!" Lee dismounted and walked to the man. The prisoner thought he was about to be shot, but Lee inquired as to the man's wounds. Then Lee said, "My son, I hope you will soon be well."

The Confederate wounded had a hard ride south, for in the retreat many ambulances had to travel across country. Meade's wounded were cared for in Gettysburg and in nearby farm-houses.

More than fifty-one thousand men had been killed, wounded, or were missing (the Confederate side alone lost 28,000) in the greatest battle ever fought in the Western Hemisphere.

General Lee was sad, but he shouldered the blame for the defeat. "This is *my* fault," he said. "I am the one who lost the fight." In reality, the Southerners had lost because their leaders had not seized opportunities.

Chapter 20

THE ROCK OF CHICKAMAUGA

A FTER the Battle of Gettysburg, many Yankees believed their armies could coast to victory, but almost at once a shadow fell across the North, for bad rioting broke out in New York City.

A huge mob, led by agitators, protested against the drafting of men into the armed services. The mob looted and burned stores in the big city. It attacked Negroes, beating many to death, and even set fire to a Negro orphan asylum. Troops, including the famous New York 7th Regiment and the West Point cadets, were rushed to the scene. They stopped the riots, but almost two million dollars' worth of damage had been done.

Now the heavy fighting shifted away from Pennsylvania and Virginia to Tennessee. In the desolate woods along the winding Chickamauga Creek the armies of Braxton Bragg, a Confederate. and the Union General William Rosecrans—two unusual officers —were ready to fight.

"Rosey" Rosecrans had a fine reputation in the old regular army, but he was a man who now argued over trifles, a leader who easily became confused. The Confederate Bragg was a much-hated man. Far worse, he was the kind of general who could think up fine plans but did not have the force of character to execute them. His men had little confidence in him. These were the two commanders who faced each other in the boggy and marshy country along Chickamauga Creek.

General Bragg fooled Rosey Rosecrans by sending a handful of soldiers into the Union lines. These men, who posed as deserters, told exciting tales. They said the Southern Army was in headlong flight to the rear.

Rosey could see himself and his army moving in for the kill. He marched his men forward confidently. But he was in great danger, for the Confederates lay in wait for him near West Chickamauga Creek.

Now it was Bragg's turn to make an error, and he made the favorite error of many Civil War generals: he attacked piecemeal fashion rather than attacking all along the battle line at the same time. This gave the defenders time to adjust themselves to the attack.

On the right of the Confederate line was a famous fighter, one of the best cavalrymen ever to ride in our country, General Nathan Bedford Forrest. Bedford Forrest did not have the advantage of a fine education, but he had wonderful common sense and a burning desire to *win*. Not long before this battle, at the head of 500 horsemen, he had chased the Yankee raider, Colonel Abel D. Streight, and 1,700 Union cavalrymen. Forrest, hard on Streight's heels, came to Black Creek, near Gadsden, Alabama. The daring Confederate horseman needed information as to how to get across the creek, for the Yankees had blocked the bridge.

A tawny-haired girl, Emma Sanson, climbed on the back of Forrest's gray charger. She guided Forrest to a place where he and his men could ford the stream. Rifle fire pierced the heroine's sunbonnet, but she was not hit. Emma Sanson's unusual ride enabled General Forrest to capture the Federal raider and his men.

At the Battle of Chickamauga Forrest had his men fighting on foot. He believed a man could not fire accurately enough from the back of a horse, so he often had them dismount to fight. In this battle, General Forrest made an odd picture as he fired his pistol in the front rank with his men, for he wore a linen duster.

In the thick of the battle a gap appeared in the Union line. Old Pete Longstreet, who had been sent to Tennessee by General Lee, led his men through the hole. He took with him 10,000 soldiers and six batteries of artillery. The Northern troops were now in great danger. Union troops started to withdraw to the city of Chattanooga, ten miles away. Even General Rosecrans himself moved to the city. Things looked black for the North. It appeared to be a complete rout until a great Northern leader stood his ground. This man was Major General George H. Thomas.

George Thomas had demonstrated courage when he was a cadet at West Point. Once, while a plebe at the Military Academy, an upperclassman entered Thomas' room and said he was going to haze Thomas and his roommate, William Tecumseh Sherman. Thomas said to the upperclassman, "You leave the room at once or I will throw you out the window!" Now, as a fighting general, Thomas rallied his men. With the Confederates pressing close, Thomas put what men he could get into position on Horseshoe Ridge, pulling his flanks back until his lines formed a huge U.

More Union men left the fighting for the safety of Chattanooga. Things looked black for the Union troops who stayed. Many were low on ammunition. Somebody had made the horrible mistake of sending the ammunition train to Chattanooga.

"Pap" Thomas, a heavy-set general whose square chin was covered with whiskers, looked like a kindly grandpa. When he found out about the blunder, he roared, "Take the ammunition from the dead!" His lion heart began to assert itself. He was not going to retreat. His courage helped others on the Federal side. Thirty thousand men in blue rallied along Horseshoe Ridge and fought under his orders. They withstood Confederate attacks for five minute-creeping hours.

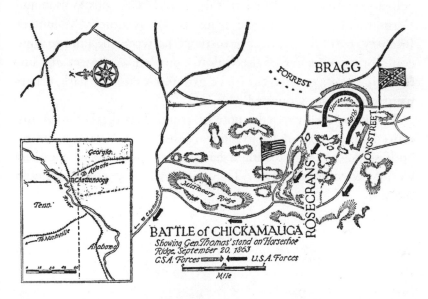

BATTLE of CHICKAMAUGA
Showing Gen. Thomas' stand on Horseshoe Ridge. September 20, 1863
C.S.A. Forces ▬▬▬ ◄▬▬ *U.S.A. Forces*
Mile

General Longstreet readied his men for a final charge against the ridge. When the Confederates ran at the Federals, the Union men shot at them with pistols and fought with swords and bayonets. Some, completely out of ammunition, swung their muskets as clubs. Many Union troops broke under the pressure and streaked for the city.

One regiment, the 19th Infantry of the regular army, had every officer either killed or wounded except the youngest second lieutenant. But this regiment, with the young officer in command, stood its ground. Right with them was General Thomas.

The Confederates were exhausted. They could do no more.

Both General Thomas and the 19th Infantry became known as the "Rock of Chickamauga" because they did not run and because they protected the rear of Rosecrans' army, saving it from an even worse defeat. Old Pap Thomas became the idol of his men.

On the battlefield, at dusk, the wounded were begging for help and were crying, "Water! Oh, water!" Captains Wilson and Wright and six of their men, from the 8th Kentucky Volunteer Infantry, carried a white flag of truce between the lines so they could bring out some of the Union wounded. A shower of Confederate bullets greeted the brave group. Later, after dark, others went out to the wounded.

The Rebel yell carried a note of triumph as the Union Army retired to the city of Chattanooga. There were heavy losses on both sides. The Confederates had lost the most men, but their victory encouraged them. They believed they could still win the war.

Chapter 21

BATTLE ABOVE THE CLOUDS
AND MISSIONARY RIDGE

◇◇

THE Union Army in the city of Chattanooga was in bad shape. The men were exhausted. No one had slept in forty-eight hours. Worse, their spirit was at rock bottom because of the defeat at Chickamauga Creek. As fatigued as the men were, the officers issued picks and shovels and had their soldiers dig rifle pits and trenches in the city. They expected attack.

But the Confederates had a different idea. They surrounded the city in a huge half-circle and fortified the high ground. The place became a trap for Rosecrans' army.

And it was a dismal trap. The Union soldiers grazed their animals on the lawns of the city and chopped down all the trees for firewood. To complete the dreary picture, the wounded began to dribble in from Horseshoe Ridge. Almost immediately food in the city began to get low.

When the rations of the soldiers were reduced, the soldiers bought food from the townspeople. Soon that source gave out. Captain Crozer wrote that he had located a sutler who was selling pies "composed of flour and water, little rank grease, with still less dried apples, and without sugar and spices of any kind. They cost twenty-five cents each." Shortly even food as poor as this was not available. The soldiers began to loot the homes for food.

One bright spot in the Union situation was General Old Pap Thomas. His stout-hearted stand on Horseshoe Ridge caught the imagination of the soldiers. They came to look at him the way Confederate privates had crowded up the Gettysburg road to look at Old Pete Longstreet.

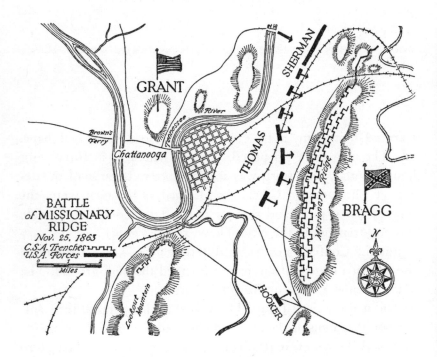

The Confederates held a splendid position. Their trenches on Lookout Mountain and on Missionary Ridge looked down on Rosecrans' army. Both mountains were tremendous obstacles. Lookout Mountain rose 1,600 feet above the valley floor, and the cliffs at the north end of Missionary Ridge were almost perpendicular to the farm land near the Tennessee River. At the back of the Union Army the curve of the river cradled the city. Confederate sharpshooters blocked the supply routes. General

Rosecrans' Union Army was cooped up and food was running dangerously low.

To make the Union position more pitiful, the Confederate cavalryman, "Fighting Joe" Wheeler, slashed into middle Tennessee and captured a wagon train of 300 wagons trying to get through to the city. Joe Wheeler, who looked and acted like a gamecock, made a bonfire of the wagons. Shortly 11,000 mules and great numbers of artillery horses in the besieged city died for want of forage, and the soldiers themselves began to starve. Sergeant Gordon, of the 44th Indiana Volunteer Infantry, told later how he received three and one-half crackers, a little corn, and three tablespoons of coffee for sixteen men. The crackers were wormy, the corn black.

In this regiment an odd character, Private Levi Wallack, liked to go on scouts by himself into enemy territory. One night, behind the enemy lines, Levi located some cattle. Although the cattle guards fired at him, Wallack succeeded in stampeding fifteen head down the ridge and into the Union lines. This made Levi Wallack a hero, and he earned three of the cattle for his friends in his regiment.

At night the Union troops could hear Confederate bands playing "Dixie." Things seemed very gay up on Missionary Ridge. They were anything but gay in Chattanooga after two months of siege.

Lincoln and his cabinet were worried, for General Rosecrans did little to help the situation. Lincoln said, "Rosecrans acts like a duck hit on the head." The President now put his best fighter, U. S. Grant, in place of Rosecrans, and promoted General Thomas to command an army under General Grant. The Union soldiers cheered Old Pap when they heard the news.

Grant looked unkempt and sloppy to some as he rode into the besieged city, but he knew how to get soldiers to fight. His first thought was of the health of his men. He ordered vegetables and beef rushed to Chattanooga, and he arranged for the supply trains to be well guarded to make certain the supplies got through.

Five days after Grant's arrival the Union soldiers were eating full rations and their morale shot up. Next, General Grant arranged for more soldiers to be brought to Chattanooga. While they were marching to him, Grant rode out to get a good look at the land over which he would have his armies fight, as he had done at Fort Donelson. He took along a guard to make certain he would not be captured.

There was no doubt in Grant's mind that he could win. He had confidence in the Union soldiers and he was not afraid.

Although the Confederates held the whip hand, things were not going well in their army up on the high ground. The reason was General Bragg.

Bragg, a tall, awkward man with deep piercing eyes, had a bright mind, but he irritated everyone about him. His men disliked him. One reason was that his punishments were unusually severe. If, in Bragg's mind, circumstances warranted, for punishment he would have a man strung up by the thumbs. He also ran true to his reputation for not taking care of his men. Food supplies were available in the rear, but little food reached the thousands of Confederate soldiers at the front. The spirit in Bragg's army continued to sag.

Braxton Bragg's officers realized that he was fumbling away a great opportunity, for he would not attack. It was obvious to his officers that General Grant would obtain reinforcements, but Bragg felt that his siege would make the Union Army surrender. Now he made a tragic blunder. He weakened his army by ordering General Pete Longstreet and 12,000 men to march a hundred miles so they could fight in Knoxville.

While Bragg weakened his army, the Northern Army grew.

General Sherman, a hard fighter, arrived at the head of a large force.

Down along the river the pickets on both sides were meeting at night on an island in the center of the river. They traded information, newspapers, and bullets. One night, a sole Yankee soldier appeared on the island, scantily dressed. He talked to the Confederates, and they liked him so much they invited him to cross over to their side of the river. The Yankee said he could not swim, so the Confederates showed him where he could wade across. That Yankee was the cavalry leader General John T. Wilder, and in the forthcoming battle he led his horsemen across the river at the ford where he had tested the depth of the water.

Soon after General Sherman brought reinforcements, General Grant ordered an attack on Lookout Mountain. Fighting Joe Hooker led a force up the rocky cliffs through the misty clouds. Grant and his staff watched from below in the valley, listening to the sounds of the battle. Finally, the clouds parted. A man on the summit of the mountain waved a flag. The officers looked through their field glasses. "That's the Stars and Stripes!" Grant said happily.

The Union bands in the valley played "Hail to the Chief" as the Confederates on the mountain pulled back to their main battle line on Missionary Ridge.

The next day Grant placed his men along the foot of the ridge in preparation for the big assault. Above, the Confederates became nervous as they watched the Federals form a battle line two miles long. The Confederates were at a disadvantage, for they could not depress their cannons enough to fire on Grant's men.

The Union Army attacked the Confederate rifle pits at the foot of the slope. "The noise," one man wrote, "sounded like 10,000 woodchoppers, and an occasional boom of a cannon would remind you of a tree falling."

Now there was a halt to re-form the Union lines. The Confederate prisoners were marched hurriedly to the rear. Sergeant Owen Shaw, a Union color-bearer, although slightly wounded, marched on up the slope. Another ball struck him in the hand, but he kept going. When he was so weak he could not climb farther, he planted the flagstaff in the ground as an inspiration for his regiment.

The Union soldiers were nervous while the blue lines were being re-formed. They were receiving rifle fire from above. The bullets were cracking and men went down. Suddenly soldiers from Kansas and Indiana moved up the slope and the whole Union line surged forward without an order from General Grant.

Grant, who was watching from below, said angrily to General Thomas, "By whose orders are those troops going up the hill?"

"Sir," replied Thomas, "it is probably their own idea."

"It's all right if it turns out all right," Grant said, "but if not, someone will suffer."

The blue line fought its way up the steep slope. Sixty color-bearers were marching in the advancing battle line. They were greeted by sheets of fire from the men in gray. At the top there was a wild battle until the Confederates broke and ran. General Bragg himself narrowly escaped capture.

It was a terrible day for the Confederates. Although he blamed his army for the defeat, Bragg had thrown away an opportunity and the South had lost an important battle. The fiery General Forrest announced he would not serve under Bragg any more. President Davis was in a quandary. He admired Bragg's brain, but Davis saw at last that General Bragg could not command an army, so he promoted Bragg and brought him to Richmond, where he served very well as an adviser.

This was the end of three hard years of warfare. In Washington, President Lincoln was happy over the victory. He telegraphed the soldiers, "God bless you all," and shortly he appointed as his commander in chief the best man in the Union armies, U. S. Grant.

Chapter 22

SAM DAVIS OF TENNESSEE

A FTER every battle, both armies had two hard problems to solve: how to take care of the wounded, and what to do with prisoners.

Many wounded on both sides died because arrangements to care for them were poor. Often the wounded were carried more than a mile from the battlefield on improvised stretchers before they received first aid. The men who carried them to the rear were usually friends in the same company. This in itself was a bad practice, because it weakened the firing line. In some battles the wounded lay on or near the battlefield for a week before being moved to a hospital.

Both sides were hard pressed for hospitals. They used anything they could—churches, warehouses, stores, tents, huts, homes, and hotels. As a rule, one surgeon had to take care of about three hundred wounded men. As in every war, the enemy wounded received attention last.

There was great suffering and, as the war rolled on, the Southern hospitals received fewer and fewer medicines because of the blockade.

Kindhearted women did their best to help care for the

wounded. Women like Elizabeth Comstock of Michigan, a preacher in the Society of Friends, and Ellen Whelan of Boston devoted themselves to nursing. Clara Barton, who had been a clerk and schoolteacher, worked to see that supplies and medicines reached the Union Army hospitals and camps. Fannie Ricketts boldly entered the Confederate lines after the First Battle of Bull Run. Her husband, a Union artillery captain, had been wounded and captured. She was determined to nurse him and she did not fear the enemy. Dorothea Lynde Dix organized a Female Nurse Corps to assist the army doctors. But there were few "angels of mercy" compared to the great number of wounded.

One strange but devoted character was Mary Ann ("Mother") Bickerdyke. People in Galesburg, Illinois, knew her worth and chose her to carry medical supplies to sick Union soldiers at Cairo. She helped in the hospital and had no fear of army regulations—or officers. One day in the Cairo hospital an inspecting lieutenant delayed a meal that Mother had prepared for her sick. She waited until she lost patience, then marched up to the inspector. His blouse was partly open. Mother spied an undershirt that was marked with NWSC, which meant it had been sent for the use of patients by the Northwestern Sanitary Commission. She threw the lieutenant down and ripped his shirt off and was on the way to examining his underpants when a brother officer came to his rescue.

On another occasion Mother's pies were disappearing from the kitchen. This made her angry, because she had cooked the pies for the soldiers who were recovering from illness and wounds. She made some "decoy" pies and placed them where the thieves could find them. She returned later to find the men who had stolen the pies very sick. "This is just a hint," Mother warned.

In Richmond and other Southern cities and towns it was

fashionable for women to nurse the wounded. Some even helped with the sick and wounded prisoners, but this task was not popular.

The treatment of prisoners of war was a black mark against both sides. The top leaders found themselves involved in a vicious circle. Escaped prisoners would tell of the poor food and harsh treatment they had received and, as a result, the prisoners at hand were treated more meanly.

After a battle, the prisoners were marched to the rear and usually to a railroad. Particularly on the Southern side they were often herded into boxcars and the doors were closed and locked. At times they traveled with little food or water.

Captain Wilkins, of the 112th Illinois, a prisoner of the Confederates, wrote: "... Four of us cut a hole in the railroad car and jumped. One man, Lieutenant Griffin, was too weak to travel. We shook hands with him with tears in our eyes and left him. The Negroes helped us. They fed us and guided us through swamps, bogs, forests, over hills and mountains. We got back to the Union lines at Dalton, Georgia. There I wrote my wife."

Near Savannah, when conditions were tense, the Southerners got the idea of starving prisoners into taking the Confederate Oath of Allegiance, then making them serve in the Confederate Army. But this idea produced worthless soldiers, because they deserted at the first chance.

One of the most notorious prisons was at Andersonville, Georgia, where more than thirty-three thousand Union soldiers were herded into thirty acres. Harsh guards patrolled an enclosure where the prisoners were without shelter. To avoid cold winds, they burrowed into the earth like animals. Their only water came from a polluted stream that ran through the camp. Each day they received a little beef of the poorest grade and some meal, made by grinding corn and corncobs together. To get more food, the prisoners were forced to sell what few possessions they had to the guards. There was no soap, no issue of clothing to replace worn-out garments, no sanitation, and little medical attention from Confederate authorities. The dead were hauled out by the wagonload, and those who survived looked like skeletons. In this prison camp more than twelve thousand men died.

Libby Prison, a former tobacco warehouse in Richmond, was almost as bad. If a prisoner showed himself at a window he could expect to be shot at by the guards. The crowded condition and the lack of sanitation made the place almost unbearable. The food was only slightly better than at Andersonville. Boxes for the prisoners, arriving at the rate of three hundred a week, were opened by the guards before the prisoners' eyes and the contents stolen.

Edward Penstone, a young soldier from Illinois, shot in the arm at the Battle of Chickamauga, was captured and shipped by freight train to Atlanta and thence to Richmond. At the capital of the Confederacy he was placed in a prison hospital where he was fortunate to receive nursing care from Southern women. But he received only a pint of thin bean soup a day, a small piece of meat, and a slice of bread. One night two of his friends made a ladder, by tearing up blankets, and lowered themselves from a window. Edward could not go with them because his arm was in a sling. The next day he caught the wrath of the prison officials because there had been an escape. Several months later he was exchanged, after he had signed a paper and taken an oath that he would never again fight against the Confederacy.

Yankee prisoners at Salisbury, North Carolina, somehow got enough athletic equipment to enable them to pass the time playing baseball. The umpire, a dignified authority, wielded a cane and sat in a chair behind home plate.

Great numbers of prisoners were not exchanged because both sides mistrusted each other. They feared prisoners who were able to fight again would break their parole as soon as they were freed.

Northern prison camps were also horrible. In the Union camps along the Great Lakes, the Confederate prisoners suffered from exposure and many died of lung ailments.

Near Chicago, at Camp Douglas, 10,000 Confederates were crowded into seventeen acres. One lady of Chicago, the wealthy Mrs. Mary Blackburn Morris, did what she could by supplying food for the hungry men. Once a party of visiting Englishmen came to this camp. They wanted to see Confederate soldiers and how the Yankees took care of them. When the prisoners were lined up they chanted, "Bread! Bread! Bread!" This embarrassed the Union officers in charge and they cut out the bread ration for twenty-four hours and would let no one bring the men food.

Twenty-two hundred Confederate prisoners died at Camp Chase, Ohio. Stories of starvation in the camp made the South bitter.

The fearless Colonel John H. Morgan, cavalry leader from Kentucky, had earned the nickname "The Rebel Raider." With his black pointed beard, wide mustache, and flaring hat, he looked like a swordsman of old France. He was captured while leading a raid through Indiana and Ohio and was thrown into the Ohio State Penitentiary. He and a number of his officers had their beards and heads shaved to show them they were regarded as jailbirds. Thoughts of escape filled Morgan's mind, just as they do that of any prisoner. In prison, leaders come to the front as they do elsewhere. Colonel Morgan organized his men. They tunneled out of their cells and reached the Southern lines.

Confederate prisoners of war, thousands of them, were placed in pens at Point Lookout, Maryland. This prison camp was on ten acres of flat sand, a few inches above high tide. No cover of any kind existed. The drinking water was scarce and unpalatable. The problem of how to put in time was almost as bad as the problem of living on scanty rations. When the weather got cold, the men were given tents, fifteen feet in diameter. Eighteen men were expected to live in a tent.

Anthony Keiley, a Virginian, was shifted from Point Lookout to Elmira Prison in New York. Here he found thousands and thousands of other Confederates. Sick and wounded prisoners were begging for potato peelings to keep alive. The death rate, Keiley reported (386 men dying the first month he was there), was higher than at Andersonville.

The prison camp at Elmira was neat and orderly, but hundreds died from "homesickness" (it was recorded) and the bitterness of a northern New York winter. An inspector wrote, "... Those in tents suffer. There are no stoves in quarters or hospital." The colonel in command of the camp endorsed the report: "Many men are in tents without stoves or blankets."

Not many escaped from the watchful eyes of the Union guards at Elmira, but John Fox Maull of the Jeff Davis Artillery of Selma, Alabama, tried. Fox Maull's plan of tunneling had to be kept quiet even from fellow prisoners, for fear someone would talk too much. The ten members of the escaping gang took an oath to keep the plan of escape secret. The penalty for breaking the oath would be a knife in the back.

The prisoners stole a spade from a contractor. Putegnat, a prisoner in on the plot, gave his woolen shirt to be made into bags to carry away the dirt to a different part of the camp each night. To fool the guards, the prisoners above the tunnel got a piece of tin and hammered on it to conceal the noise of the digging. They told the guards they were making spoons.

As the night of the escape drew near, the prisoners became nervous. They could picture the arms of their loved ones at home waiting for them. A little bit remained to be dug in the eighty-foot tunnel when they hit a fencepost. They dug around it and got out, only to discover guards close by. Fortunately, it was pitch black and the guards did not see them.

Luckily for the escaped prisoners, they blundered into the home of a man and his wife who helped them get away. Many people in the town of Elmira felt sorry for the prisoners and were generally sympathetic. Five of the ten reached home safely. The story of what happened to the five who did not arrive is not known. When John Fox Maull told his tale of the escape, the Montgomery (Alabama) *Advertiser* headlined: THRILLING STORY OF TEN BRAVE CONFEDERATES' ESCAPE FROM THE HORRORS OF THE MILITARY PRISON AT ELMIRA.

The life in prison camps on both sides was a blot on our nation. It is hard to believe Americans could be so brutal.

One of the worst incidents involving a prisoner took place in the little town of Pulaski, Tennessee, when Private Sam Davis, a nineteen-year-old Southern soldier, was captured.

Sam Davis looked like an average American country boy. He had a pleasant, bronzed face and straight black hair. He was a member of the 1st Tennessee Regiment and was on detached duty with Coleman's Scouts when captured. The Union soldiers found a map in his saddle giving information about Federal forces and fortifications in middle Tennessee.

Sam Davis was court-martialed and found guilty of being a spy and of carrying information that would help the enemies of the United States.

"*I am not a spy*," he said.

The court of officers sentenced the young soldier to die a spy's death by hanging.

The people in the town pointed out to General Granville M. Dodge that young Sam Davis did not violate the rules of war by wearing civilian clothing. Davis had on the Confederate butternut-gray uniform, with several Confederate brass buttons on his jacket. The townsmen said he should be treated as an ordinary prisoner of war. But the Yankee general did not set the sentence aside.

As the day approached, General Dodge began to worry about executing Davis. "Tell me," the general said to the young man, "where you got the secret information on the map, and we will not hang you."

Sam's answer was one of the great sentences of American history. *"If I had a thousand lives,"* he said, *"I would lose them all here before I would betray my friends."*

A scaffold was built for the hanging on a hill so that it could be seen all over town. The fatal day arrived. Sam Davis was placed in a wagon, seated on his coffin, and paraded through the streets. A silence hung over the town. Even the Union troops were depressed over the fate that faced the young Confederate soldier.

On the hill, Davis was seated near the scaffold. The noose in the new rope hanging from the top of the scaffold swung gently in the breeze. Captain Armstrong and Captain Chickasaw, of the Union Army, again offered Davis his life if he would only tell who gave him the plans and information. Davis said nothing.

General Dodge walked up. "It is not too late," the general pleaded. "Tell me who helped you obtain the secret information and you will be taken to the Confederate lines and freed."

"I cannot," Sam replied. "How long have I to live?"

"Fifteen minutes," the general answered. The Union general was shaken. He had thought that, in the shadow of the scaffold, Davis would break down and tell, but he did not.

Captain Armstrong, in charge of the hanging, shook his head. "I hate to do this," he said. "I would almost rather die myself."

Sam Davis mounted the scaffold.

"I am prepared to die," he said, "but I am innocent." He took one last look at the sun. The rope was fastened about his neck and he was hanged. But echoing through the halls of history is Sam Davis' testament of loyalty: "If I had a thousand lives, I would lose them all before I would betray my friends."

◇◇◇

Chapter 23

WAR IN THE FORESTS
AND UNDERGROUND

◇◇◇

GENERAL U. S. GRANT, the new commander in chief of the
Federal armies under President Lincoln, was certain he
could defeat Robert E. Lee. Sam Grant decided the only way to
do this was to attack and keep on attacking. He explained his
plan to Lincoln and the President approved. They planned that
all of the Union armies would eventually meet and fight Lee's
Army of Northern Virginia.

The appointment of Sam Grant as the senior general buoyed
up the Union Army. The soldiers knew he had bulldog determination and courage. A smart observer in the 6th Wisconsin
wrote home, ". . . Grant holds the life of the Nation almost in his
own hands. God help him and our country!"

Grant was not flashy. The Union soldiers did not greet him
with cheers and applause as he rode among them as they had
George McClellan, but they realized Grant knew his job. They
believed he would be the leader who could end the war with
victory.

To give Lee battle, General Grant marched his huge army into
the Wilderness. This was the same gloomy area through which
the armies had fought a year before.

Lee boldly decided to attack even though Grant's army was twice as large as his own. Because the Confederate scouts knew the roads and trails better than they had a year before, the graying Southern leader felt confident. But it would not be easy. He no longer had Stonewall Jackson, and the man at the head of the Union Army was not the vacillating General Hooker.

Almost 200,000 men fought in the dense forests and thickets of the Wilderness. Officers could not keep in touch with their men. It was difficult for either side to avoid piecemeal attacks.

In the first battle of the Wilderness the Confederates had lost Stonewall Jackson. Now General "Pete" Longstreet was shot accidentally in the neck by his own men. He was carried to the rear and General Lee took over Longstreet's job of leading in close combat against the Yankees. The Texans did not like this. "Go back, General Lee!" they shouted. "Go back!" But this had no effect on Lee. He was fearless.

Again the woods and underbrush caught on fire. Hundreds of wounded were burned to death despite brave efforts on both sides to rescue them.

Neither side won. But Grant was not disheartened as other Federal generals had been after a fight with Lee. On the contrary, Sam Grant wanted a chance to fight in more open country, so he pushed toward Spotsylvania Court House. He hoped this would enable him to cut Lee off from his greatest source of supplies, Richmond.

Jeb Stuart, the dashing Confederate cavalryman, while on a scout, discovered that Grant's huge supply train of 4,000 wagons was moving, and he sent this information as fast as he could to Lee. The great Confederate guessed that Grant was going to Spotsylvania. He ordered Jeb and the cavalry to slow Grant up so he could get there first.

Jeb Stuart carried out Lee's orders, but things were difficult because Grant had improved the Union cavalry. Sam Grant had not liked the way the horsemen had been used in the past. Other Union generals fighting Lee had used the cavalry as wagon-train guards, on small scouts behind the enemy lines, as mounted messengers, and as pickets—that is, on outpost duty. Sam Grant believed his 12,000 well-equipped horsemen should be a weapon. He selected "Little Phil" Sheridan and made him chief of cavalry and said, "You stop the raids of Jeb Stuart."

WILDERNESS TO PETERSBURG

C.S.A ⟹ ⟸ U.S.A

Miles

Washington

Wilderness
Fredericksburg
Spotsylvania
Charlottesville
Hanover C.H.
Yellow Tavern
LEE
GRANT
Richmond
Cold Harbor
Appomattox C.H.
Petersburg
Five Forks
Potomac R.
Rappahannock River
York River
James River
Chesapeake Bay
Atlantic Ocean

Sheridan, a small, dynamic, hotheaded Irishman from Ohio, was the man for the job. He had never avoided a fight. In fact, in his West Point cadet days he had almost been discharged from the Academy for fighting an upperclassman.

Phil Sheridan led his Union cavalry in a slash behind the Confederates and raised Cain in Lee's rear. He destroyed two locomotives and a hundred railroad cars, as well as many horses and mules. The loss of the horses and mules hurt the Confederates because they were already short of animals.

In a cavalry fight at Yellow Tavern, the gallant Confederate cavalry leader, Jeb Stuart, received a pistol burst in the stomach. The men with Stuart placed him gently in a mule-drawn ambulance and started toward Richmond. President Jefferson Davis heard the news of the wounding of the famous cavalryman and rushed to see him. It was obvious that General Jeb Stuart was dying—even Stuart himself knew it. He started giving his equipment away. "... I leave my sword to my son," he said. Then he asked the men about him to sing the hymn "Rock of Ages."

When Lee heard of Stuart's death he said sadly, "Jeb Stuart was second to none in bravery...."

Grant arrived at Spotsylvania to find Robert E. Lee already there and his men behind breastworks. The popular Major General John Sedgwick of Grant's army went out to inspect the lines. Sedgwick had a lighthearted manner which the Union soldiers liked. He often teased the men in a way that amused them, and he knew how to lead. At one point in his tour he stopped to talk to a private. A bullet whiz-cracked overhead and the private ducked to the ground. General Sedgwick laughed. "I'm ashamed of you," he said. "You can't dodge a bullet! Besides, they couldn't hit an elephant at this distance."

"I believe in dodging," answered the soldier.

The general laughed again and ordered the soldier to his place. At that instant a Confederate sharpshooter took careful aim at General Sedgwick and shot him dead.

The fighting at Spotsylvania was as vicious as the clash in the Wilderness. At one place the Confederate lines jutted out toward the Yankees. The Confederates called this salient "The Mule's Shoe," but soon after the fighting started they renamed the ninety-degree turn in the trenches the "Bloody Angle."

Daringly the Union artillerymen ran their field pieces forward by hand within close range of the enemy. The men in gray quickly called for more artillery to quell the Yankee batteries. At the moment when the fighting became hand to hand, the terrible canister ripped into the Yankees. The Union men rallied. Horses and cannoneers at the Confederate guns were shot down. The fighting at the Bloody Angle lasted sixteen hours.

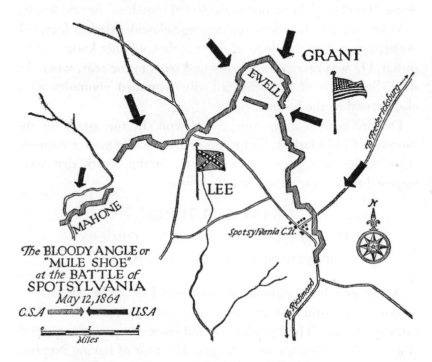

The BLOODY ANGLE or "MULE SHOE" at the BATTLE of SPOTSYLVANIA May 12, 1864

C.S.A ━━━➤ ◄━━━ U.S.A

Miles

Lee won at Spotsylvania because he arranged his forces better and because General Grant attacked in piecemeal fashion. But the Southern general paid a high price: 5,000 Confederates were killed, wounded, or missing. A thought entered men's minds: "How many more such victories can Lee stand?"

Grant had his army begin another circling movement to try to cut off General Lee from Richmond. The two armies met at Cold Harbor, a few miles from the Confederate capital. Before the battle, the 57th Massachusetts Regiment got ready to attack. It was a nervous moment. Private Edward Schneider, a seventeen-year-old student from Phillips Academy at Andover, marched near the head of his regiment as it moved into position. Through the pine woods he could see the Confederate fortifications. "I will be the first one in the Rebel trenches," he said firmly.

When the attack order came, young Schneider dashed forward. As he sprinted up the slope of the trenches, a bullet knocked him down. He was carried to the hospital tents in the rear, where he died. Soon 650 of Schneider's badly wounded comrades were also carried to the hospital tents.

Despite such Yankee spirit, Lee won. In the attack in the woods at Cold Harbor, Grant lost 10,000 men in twelve minutes. This terrific loss gave the newspapers in the North that were opposed to the war a chance to headline:

GRANT A BUTCHER!
HE ACTS UNDER LINCOLN'S ORDERS!
ELECT McCLELLAN PRESIDENT

Many people thought the South would never be beaten.

But such sentiments and losses did not stop the team of Lincoln and Grant. The President rushed more troops to the general. Two of the regiments were Negro. The idea of having Negroes used against them infuriated the Southerners.

Thousands of slaves were trekking into the Union lines. The Northern newspapers applauded this, but it gave the Union generals a problem, because the Negroes had to be fed.

To carry the war further into Virginia, Grant ordered a pontoon bridge built across the James River. His engineers achieved the remarkable feat of building this bridge in eight hours. Its length, 2,100 feet, made it one of the longest pontoon bridges of all time. One hundred and one boats were used to support it.

The two armies met again, this time at Petersburg, Virginia, and here General Grant lay siege to the Confederate Army. Both sides began to dig trenches.

Samuel Moulton, of the 9th New Hampshire Regiment, wrote to his brother Augustus, at Freedom, New Hampshire:

> Battle Field on Gen. Grants Right
> June 9, 1864

I arrived here yesterday afternoon and found the 9th New Hampshire Regerment in front line of Battle in the Fortifications and their Pickets out of site in another line of Rifle Pitts. The Joney Rebs sends their bulets once in a while over us and last night as our men were cutting Trees and Fortifying, The Joney Rebs come out of the woods in line of Battle but our Pickets quick drove them in again. The Pickets are firing quite constance. I expect them to go on tonight.

There is only 18 men left in Co. 'K,' inCluding Capt. Cooper. ... Most of the men lost out of the 9th N.H. regerment were killed in 5 minets by their standing their ground while another Regerment run, and the Joney Rebs come in and flanked the 9 N.H. So the 4 Companeys on the left was cut up badly and had to retreat but took the Ground back again the next day and buried some of the dead.

The slow siege warfare now began in painstaking fashion, both sides digging more trenches and building more fortifications. Sam Grant brought up tremendous siege guns and mortars and pounded the Confederate works. Soon food became scarce in Petersburg but the Petersburg *Express* said, "We can stand a siege like this for twenty years."

The Southern people were not disheartened. They still believed that the great Robert E. Lee would lead them to a victory so decisive that the Northerners would quit, and Lee himself believed this would happen.

The siege at Petersburg dragged on. At night, when their officers could not see them, Union and Confederate pickets on outguard duty met between the lines and traded coffee, tobacco, and newspapers.

Holding the south side of the city was an unusual Confederate general, Billy Mahone, a graduate of the Virginia Military Institute. Billy Mahone was five feet five inches tall and weighed less than a hundred pounds. He wore a big felt hat, a long black beard, and huge cavalry boots. He liked milk and, to make certain that he got it, he had a milch cow led wherever his troops went. Mahone not only got milk from the cow, but on marches he had cooking utensils and other equipment strapped to the animal's back. Billy Mahone had started in the war as a lieutenant colonel, but Lee, recognizing his leadership, had gradually promoted him until at Petersburg Billy wore the stars of a major general and commanded a division.

In the Union Army facing the besieged city young Lieutenant Colonel Henry Pleasants had a daring idea. In his 48th Pennsylvania Regiment he had a number of miners. Pleasants himself had considerable mining experience, having sunk several shafts in the Allegheny coal regions. Young Pleasants' idea was to tunnel under a part of the Confederate fortifications and blow up a key battery.

The plan was approved and the work started. They had only crude hand tools, and many of the men had never been in a mine, yet Pleasants convinced them they could do the job. The Pennsylvanians carried the dirt out in cracker boxes. They overcame many other obstacles, but one almost stopped them. As the shaft went farther and farther underground toward the Confederate fort, it became harder for the men working in the tunnel to get fresh air. Pleasants built a chimney and started a fire at its foot. The hot air created a draft that circulated air, and the work went on.

The Confederates could hear the digging. They guessed the Federals were tunneling under them to plant a mine, but no one knew where. The Confederates dug a number of deep holes, but they could not locate the shaft.

When the tunnel had gone 511 feet, Pleasants packed the forward end with powder. The plan was that when the mine exploded certain Union troops would rush through the gap into the Confederate works.

The big day came. The men of the 48th who had worked so hard were excited. The powder was timed to blow up at 3:30 A. M. Colonel Pleasants lit the fuse. The minutes ticked by. Nothing happened.

This was a puzzle. No one was certain what was wrong. It would be extremely dangerous for anyone to go into the mine to find what had occurred. Two volunteers stepped forward, Lieutenant Jacob Douty and the faithful soldier-miner, Sergeant Harry Reese. They said they would go into the shaft. The men of the 48th held their breath as the two men ran into the black tunnel and disappeared.

The lieutenant and the sergeant found that the fuse had burned out at a place where it had been spliced. They set the fuse on fire again and scrambled for safety.

The resulting explosion under the Confederate battery was tremendous.

Union troops, including a brigade of Negro soldiers, poured through the gap at the Confederates. There was confusion and poor leadership in the Union ranks. The Confederates quickly recovered from the surprise of the explosion and fought back. General Lee sent for Billy Mahone.

Billy Mahone's men charged into the Yankees, flags flying, the cold steel of their bayonets flashing in the blazing sun. That morning Billy Mahone's men charged three times. Their work and the firing of the Confederate artillery were too much for the Yankees, and they fell back with heavy losses. The Negro brigade alone lost 913.

Samuel Moulton wrote home after the "Battle of the Crater":

> Battlefield in Frunt of
> Petersburge, Va.,
> July, 31, 1864

... There was hot work here yesterday. Our folks maid a charge as soon as we could see in the Morning. We had 2 of the Rebels Fortes Dug under and Powder to Blow them up. There was 6 Hundred Rebels in the Forte. The Most, or at least 4 Hundred of them, must have been Blowed up and Beried in the dirt when our Regerment charged over into the Forte.

Some of the Rebes were all Beried except their heads and crying for Help, and some beried head down and their legs flying and kicking over. The 9th was the first Regerment in the Forte. They took a good many prisoners. But the 4, or Negrow Division ... swerved too far to the left. Some of the New men had never been in a fight before, and come rite in Our Brigade and piled in 10 deep. The Rebes had them in a Cross Fire and made a charge and took a good meny of Our men prisoners. The 9th lost 37 men and have 80 left to bar armes. Not a Field Officer is left in our Brigade.

Send me some letters, stamps, and newspapers. ...

The siege wore on, month after month. The two great generals began to "maneuver" by building more and more trenches and fortifications. The brilliance of Lee kept Grant from gaining a fast victory at Petersburg.

Chapter 24

TROUBLE IN THE SHENANDOAH VALLEY

WHILE Lee and Grant were at the Bloody Angle, Union General Franz Sigel marched confidently up the Shenandoah Valley. With the heavy-set general rode his large staff, and not far away trotted a cavalry escort. General Sigel had once headed a force against Stonewall Jackson in the beautiful Valley, but he had not been successful; now he commanded 7,000 veterans and expected to win.

News of Sigel's advance sped ahead. At the Virginia Military Institute a drummer beat the long roll. Out of the barracks poured the young cadets. What they had longed for was about to happen. Word had been received at V.M.I. that General John Imboden would attack the advancing Yankee army and he needed the cadets.

The V.M.I. cadets were between sixteen and eighteen years of age. It had been hard for them to study while their fathers and brothers were fighting the Yankees. Each boy looked forward to the chance to show his family what the V.M.I. Corps could do.

The cadets marched toward General Imboden under command of one of their professors. It was pouring rain; nevertheless, they hiked eighteen miles in the mud and made camp in the rain. The next day they marched twenty more miles, the following day fifteen, which brought them to New Market, Virginia.

At one in the morning, in a rainstorm, a despatch bearer arrived with the message that the cadets were to come at once to Shirley's Hill. Captain Frank Preston led the boys in prayer, then marched them through the night toward the enemy.

The cadet artillery joined the Confederate artillery. The cadet infantry battalion received orders to wait until the afternoon. During this wait they were shelled by Union artillery and two boys died. The cadets were amazed to see Confederate officers round up at pistol point Confederate skulkers—men who had deserted their companies. The cadets could not understand how a man could desert his unit.

When word was at last received for the corps to form line and fire at the enemy, the cadets took position along a rail fence and opened up. Now came a message for the cadets to team with the 62d Virginia and charge.

Not a boy quailed. The enemy was one hundred and fifty yards away across a muddy field. The cadets tore at the Yankees and the men in blue ran. This was the high point of the fight. Eight more cadets gave their lives. Sigel's Union army retreated down the Valley, the Southern boys capturing from sixty to a hundred men.

While this was not one of the great battles, the V.M.I. cadets behaved bravely under fire and enhanced the reputation of their famous school. This victory had immediate importance, for it saved the wheat crop for General Lee.

While Lee and Grant were fighting in the woods at Cold Harbor, Major General David Hunter stormed up the Shenandoah at the head of 16,000 Union troops.

As soon as he could spare troops from Petersburg, General

Lee sent the hard fighter, Lieutenant General Jubal Early, to the beautiful Valley. Early was practicing law in his home state of Virginia when the war began. He had voted against Virginia's leaving the Union, but when the war started Early became a Yankee hater. He was a bold soldier.

Early was six feet tall. His scraggly beard and a slight stoop made him look older than he was. His men dubbed him "Old Jube" and "Old Jubilee," but they stayed out of his way as much as possible, for he had a salty tongue and a quick temper.

To clear General Hunter and his army out of the Shenandoah Valley, Old Jube placed his army across the roads that were being used to supply the Union men. This caused the Yankee general to leave the Valley in a near panic, but not until his men had set fire to V.M.I. and had looted many homes.

Old Jube now started northward to carry the war across the Potomac. He figured this would ease the pressure on Lee. With Early traveled two great leaders, John B. Gordon and John C. Breckinridge. They were the type men would follow anywhere. Although Early himself was a fine leader, he needed such generals, for many of his men were marching without shoes.

At Hagerstown, Maryland, Early's cavalry collected $20,000 from the citizens. Jubal Early made it a case of "pay or have your city burned." Three days later he met and defeated a makeshift, hurriedly put together Union Army near Frederick, Maryland.

Northern newspapers yelled for protection against the Rebel raider. The papers put all the pressure they could on Lincoln, and the President wired Grant to send men at once to protect Washington. As Early's men marched for the capital, thousands in the city became nervous.

One of the men who went to the outskirts of the city to look at Old Jube's army was a tall man in a black stovepipe hat. The defenses around the city were manned with government clerks, Union soldiers who were recovering from wounds, soldiers on leave, almost anybody who could man a gun. It was an exciting time. The man in the stovepipe hat came under fire, and they pulled him down. The men did not wish to see a bullet strike their beloved President Lincoln.

But General Early decided not to attack. His soldiers were exhausted, the July sun was very hot, and he had word that powerful forces were on the way to the capital from Grant. So Early returned to the Valley, but he sent his cavalry first to Chambersburg, Pennsylvania.

Here the Confederate cavalry demanded $500,000 of the townspeople. The citizens would not pay. They said bravely that even if they had the money they would not give it. One officer of Virginia cavalry, Colonel William Peters, protested. He did not like warfare against women and children. He was placed under arrest by the Confederate brigadier general, John McCousland, and almost all of the city was burned.

Such goings-on by the men from the Valley spelled "trouble." In addition to Early and his army, the young ranger, John Mosby, was galloping at night on Shenandoah's roads, a threat to anyone who wore a blue uniform.

President Lincoln had enough of this, so he told Grant to send an army to the Valley. Grant chose one of his best soldiers, Little Phil Sheridan, for the job. He gave General Sheridan enough cavalry and foot troops so that he would outnumber General Jubal Early's men by the big margin of three to one. Grant told Sheridan to be cautious when he first went into the Valley until he knew the situation.

Sheridan was an odd-looking officer. He wore a blue coat that stretched to his knees. Its overlarge collar made him appear ill at ease. He was anything but that. He said he would not only destroy the Confederates but that he would devastate the Valley so badly that "a crow flying over it would have to carry its own rations"—which was a saying of General Grant's.

The Confederates in the Valley were in high spirits—far from frightened. Captain Dickert wrote about the 3d South Carolina Infantry's being placed on night picket duty on the Opequan River at the northern end of the Valley. The men knew the enemy was close by. Nevertheless, the Southern soldiers began to imitate a fox hunt. They howled, barked, and yelped as they marched along the river trail. Some imitated fox-hunting horns. Others encouraged the "dogs" with fox-hunting cries like, "Go to it, Joe!" "Catch 'em, Rock!" "Drive him in, boy!" and so on. The woods and ravines resounded with the cries of a hunt. Officers of the regiment could not quiet the men who were enjoying the "chase," wondering what the Yankees would think of a fox hunt at the front in time of war.

There were no jokes on Sheridan's side. He maneuvered slowly, taking time to plunder the lower end of the Valley. He wrote, "I have destroyed over two thousand barns filled with wheat and hay . . . over seventy mills filled with wheat and flour . . . I have driven in front of this army over 4,000 head of stock and have killed and issued to the troops over 3,000 sheep." Then, when two of his men were murdered, he burned every house within five miles.

To get information about Mosby's Rangers and about Early's men, General Sheridan dressed one hundred volunteers in Confederate uniform and sent them into the enemy lines. Several of these brave men were caught and hanged.

It was hard for spies and scouts to get information on the will-o'-the-wisp Mosby, but General Sheridan stopped worrying about the raider, for he realized that when the Valley was cleaned out Mosby would be hard put for hiding places.

Finding out about Jubal Early's intentions was difficult because

Early moved constantly. Old Jube did this to make Phil Sheridan think the small Southern Army was greater than it really was.

Suddenly Little Phil attacked and overwhelmed Early at Winchester. The news of the victory helped win votes for Lincoln. Congress gave Phil a gold sword, and the President wired: "God bless you."

Phil Sheridan now literally set the Valley on fire. A crow would have had to carry double rations to fly across the Shenandoah. U. S. Grant ordered Sheridan to move up the Valley and cut a railroad the Confederates were using to supply Lee with food.[1] But Sheridan was hesitant about moving, even though his army outnumbered Early's and had the benefit of the new Spencer repeating carbine.

Old Jube had a keen sense of humor. In one battle, in 1862, he saw his men advance under heavy artillery fire. At the same time one of his chaplains ran for the rear. Early stopped the chaplain and said, "Where are you going?"

"To a place of safety," was the answer.

The general said, "I have known you for thirty years. You have been trying to get to heaven, and now that you have the chance you are running. I am surprised at you, sir."

Once Stonewall Jackson had written asking *why* there were so many stragglers in the rear of Early's division. Many were afraid to tease Stonewall, but not Jubal Early. He wrote back:

Colonel A. G. Pendleton,
Ass't. Adjutant General

Colonel: Please inform General Jackson that he saw so many stragglers in rear of my division probably because he rode in rear of my division.

Respectfully,
Jubal A. Early
Commanding Division

[1] See map, Chapter 4.

But in the Valley in 1864 there was little for Early to be amused at. He drove his men harder and harder. He decided to attack Phil Sheridan's army even though it greatly outnumbered his.

In order to find how to attack the Federals, the reliable General Gordon climbed high up Massanutten Mountain. He saw at once the best route and the best place for the attack on the Union camp. General Early approved Gordon's plan and the Confederates surprised their enemy at Cedar Creek.

Phil Sheridan was at Winchester, twenty miles away. When he got news of the battle, he mounted his huge black horse, Rienzi, and rode at breakneck speed to the fight. Rienzi, named for a leader in ancient Rome, was equal to the severe journey.

When Sheridan arrived near the battle, he found his soldiers scattered on the road in panicky, terror-stricken confusion. Little Phil galloped past the ambulances and supply wagons, and Rienzi carried him over a rail fence. Sheridan stood in his stirrups, waved his cap, and yelled, "Turn, men! We are going back!" His magnetic leadership saved the day. He was aided by the poor work of the Confederates, for many of them had stopped to eat and plunder in the Union camp. With Sheridan leading, the Union men turned about and counterattacked fiercely, driving General Early's soldiers far up the Valley.

With the fortunes of war running against them, many in Jubal Early's army deserted and went home. Enemies of his in Richmond demanded that Early be relieved of his command. This was a hard thing for Lee to do, for Old Jube was devoted to the Southern cause; he was a fine fighter, and he and Lee were friends. General Lee retained him as long as he could, but when the pressure got greater and when Phil Sheridan finally won again over the small army, Jubal Early was sent home to await orders.

Sheridan's Valley campaign put an end to the Confederate forces in that part of Virginia. Little Phil was an inspiring leader, but he did faster work later when serving directly under U. S. Grant.

Chapter 25

SHERMAN'S LONG FIGHT
TO ATLANTA

WHILE Phil Sheridan was burning the Shenandoah Valley and Grant was fighting in the Wilderness, General William Tecumseh Sherman left Missionary Ridge with 105,000 Union veterans and headed for Atlanta.

Ahead of the huge Union Army, and doing his best to slow it up, was "Little Joe" Johnston. General Johnston had 65,000 Confederates. He was one of the South's leading generals. He had a magnetic personality, a friendly smile, and a jaunty all-is-well air although he had been wounded ten times. All but a few Southerners respected his ability as a leader. In that very few was Jefferson Davis. There was no love lost between the President and Johnston. The things that made "Little Joe" popular, as well as the fact that he was touchy and temperamental, irritated Jeff Davis.

General Sherman ("Uncle Billy," his men sometimes called him) was restless, full of energy. Sometimes he would walk at night with the sentry who paced up and down guarding his tent. At times William Sherman was witty, on other occasions sarcastic. He was a sandy-haired, tall, lean-cut soldier from Ohio, and his sharp nose and chin matched his personality.

At the head of William Sherman's armies rode three fine generals: George Thomas (The Rock); the serious John M. Schofield; and the handsome, knightlike Jim McPherson. McPherson had been honor man in his class at West Point. He was popular with his troops and made a striking picture on his black horse.

At the start of the campaign to Atlanta, Uncle Billy ordered that the baggage wagons be reduced to two to a regiment and said they would carry cooking utensils, not officers' baggage. All extra clothing was shipped home. Some regiments carried pup tents, others no tents at all. As for food, Sherman ordered: "Give the men three days' rations and tell 'em it has to last five. They'll have to live off the country when they can." It was going to be a rough hundred miles to Atlanta. The Federals were determined to make the march, and the Southerners were equally determined to stop them.

Johnston's Confederates soon learned that by sending a few well-aimed bullets into the Yankee advance guards they could make the Federals spread out and prepare for battle. This slowed up the Union Army. It was difficult for Sherman's soldiers to know every time what Little Joe was up to. On one wooded hill would be just enough of Johnston's Confederates to make the Yankee advance guard work an hour. The next hill would have breastworks that would take a day to reduce. Sometimes the Confederates would send their cavalry on a wide sweep to strike behind the Union columns, and at other times they would smash head on into the slowly advancing army.

The Union officers encouraged their men to push ahead. Because Uncle Billy had many more soldiers, he could move around any position and bring up many men when the Confederates gave battle. Sometimes the Union soldiers would dig trenches to protect themselves, for they could still remember Chickamauga.

All this took time, which is what Little Joe hoped for. He

prayed that something would happen that would make the Union give up the war.

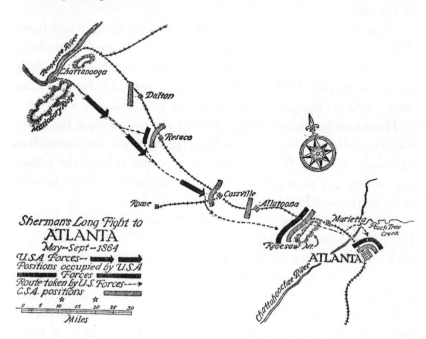

Sherman's Long Fight to
ATLANTA
May–Sept–1864
U.S.A Forces–
Positions occupied by U.S.A
Forces
Route taken by U.S. Forces---
C.S.A. positions

A big help to Sherman was the railroad that ran along the route, but to keep Sherman from using it, Johnston had his men tear up long sections of track. Here and there they burned a bridge. When the Federals found the tracks destroyed, their engineers worked fast to make repairs. The bridges were rebuilt as soon as it was safe for the bridgebuilders to go to work. The Union men could often hear the trains whistling right behind them, bringing up ammunition, other supplies, and mail from home.

As they fought their way slowly toward Atlanta, the Yankees destroyed a rich country. Fields of wheat, rye, oats, corn, and the fences about the fields were burned at every opportunity. Although gardens were raided for vegetables, the principal Yankee "dish" was hardtack. Some of Sherman's gunners wanted to know if they could put it in their cannons and shoot it in place of canister.

Living in the cold, the winds, the rain, and the heat was hard. The men on both sides did their cooking over small campfires. The Yankees melted the solder binding the two halves of their flat canteens and stuck a stick in the dish-shaped halves to make small, light frying pans, the forerunner of a later-day mess kit.

The more Sherman's armies robbed the countryside the more civilians followed his columns begging for food for themselves and their children. Sherman put out an order to stop the pillaging, saying any man caught straggling in the rear on the march, or in battle, would be shot or given hard labor.

Although it is hard for retreating troops to have high morale, Little Joe Johnston somehow kept the spirits of his men at a high level. But after the battle at Resaca, Georgia, Captain Crozer of the Iowa Infantry thought he detected a break in the Confederate spirit. He wrote his sweetheart from a camp seventy-five miles northwest of Atlanta: "At Resaca the rebs left in such a hurry they didn't even have time to bury their killed. Lots lying around in the woods.... The rebs had the best position to hold of any place. It beat Vicksburg two to one.... We have a large force and flank them every time. Some of the pickets on both sides talk to one another at night, exchanging coffee and tobacco. All my men have to exchange is leaden pills. Some nights the rebs snap caps (blanks) to make our men fire and show our position. ... I will be home on your next birthday if I am alive."

Slowly Sherman's armies ground ahead. As they neared Marietta, Georgia, his scouts informed him that the enemy had a strong position on Kenesaw Mountain.

Sherman attacked. It was a hard fight. At one time in the battle the Iowa troops lost six cannons and were ordered to go and get them. They charged against a hail of bullets. When they recaptured their guns, they saw General Sherman throw his cap into the air. The usual procedure was reversed, when the general gave a cheer for the troops.

After the battle, all of the armies worked for two days under a flag of truce burying the dead. There were 3,000 Union soldiers to be buried; a lesser number of Johnston's men. During this period of truce, a strapping Ohio soldier challenged the biggest Confederate to a wrestling match. Lieutenant Colonel Hinman, of Ohio, reported that scores of men on both sides came to watch the bout. The troops forgot for a while that they were engaged in war. The Yankee threw the Southerner three times in a row. After the white flags had been taken down, the soldiers went back to their units and the shooting began again.

General Johnston's failure to win was too much for Jeff Davis, back in Richmond. He had little patience with Joe Johnston and felt that somehow, somewhere in the long retreat from Chattanooga, Johnston should have beaten Sherman's three armies. So Davis sent Johnston a sharp note and relieved him from command. At the head of the army would be the fighter from Texas, General John B. Hood. The news of the change in command quickly reached the Union lines by deserters and prisoners.

General Sherman knew Hood had lost the use of an arm at Gettysburg and had had a leg amputated after Chickamauga, and it was common knowledge that Hood had to be strapped on his horse.

To learn what he should expect from the new commander, Sherman talked to two of his generals, Schofield and McPherson.

"Look out for a fight," the two Union generals warned Sherman. They said that Hood was a man who liked combat, that he was a gambler at heart. They said he wore a beard that made him look older than he was, and that he was about thirty-three years old. "All in all," they agreed, "John Hood is brave, determined, and rash."

Sherman was happy. He was tired of Johnston's shrewd delaying tactics that had let him advance only a little more than a mile a day. The Union Army got ready for battle.

It did not have long to wait. Two days after he had taken command, General Hood ordered his Southern army to attack. At Peachtree Creek, five miles from Atlanta, he made the mistake of ordering the brunt of the attack against the troops of Old Pap Thomas, The Rock of Chickamauga. Pap's men stood fast and Hood retired his army into the city after a hard fight with heavy losses.

At the close of the battle, a group of men carried a corpse toward General Sherman's tent. When General Sherman found that it was the body of one of his best generals and his close friend, Jim McPherson, he was so crushed he cried. McPherson had been near the head of an advancing column when the Confederates surprised it. The brilliant young leader had been killed in the first volley.

The fight from Chattanooga to Atlanta had been long and costly to both sides. Although Sherman had not destroyed Hood's army, the Union general had the Confederates shut up in the city. Sherman now lay siege to Atlanta. He strangled it, devastated it, and cut off supplies going from the Deep South to Lee at Petersburg.

Chapter 26

FULL SPEED AHEAD!

G ENERAL SHERMAN's army was showing the Union it had
Atlanta in a death grip, but millions in the North would
have been happy to see the war stop, even though the cause the
Union was fighting for had not been accomplished.

Although the Union armies were gaining victories, the cost
in lives and in sick and wounded was startling. And it was harder
to live because of the war. The cost of food, clothing, and many
other things was getting higher and higher. The dollar was buy-
ing only half of what it did when the war started; the laborer's
wages were going down. The fact that living conditions were
much worse in the Confederacy meant nothing to many.

The Northern Democrats were campaigning for *"No More
War!"* They were not worried because the Southern states were
not yet back in the Union, because much blood had been spilled,
or because millions of dollars had been spent. They wanted only
one thing: to stop the war.

Horace Greeley, the great newspaper editor, founder of the
New York *Tribune,* wanted peace regardless of the cost. He

wrote that it was impossible for Abraham Lincoln to be re-elected.

There was still talk that the Copperheads might overthrow the United States government. The traitor, Clement Vallandigham, whom Lincoln had sent South, had gone to Canada by sea, and from Canada he had returned to the United States. He was doing everything possible to stop the war and to hinder President Lincoln.

The Northern Democrats surprised the country by nominating General George McClellan to run for President against Abraham Lincoln, and McClellan accepted. The Northern Democrats spread the word that McClellan had been treated unfairly when he was commanding general of the Army of the Potomac, that thousands of his former soldiers still loved him, and their votes would put him in the White House. The Northern Democrats reasoned that because they had nominated him, he would stop the war if elected.

"What if the Confederacy does become a separate country?" asked the members of the peace party. "Maybe that is best, after all. The South does not understand us and we do not understand them."

The picture looked dark for Abraham Lincoln and his hopes for a united country.

Suddenly there was news from Mobile Bay.

Admiral David Farragut, the hero of the Battle of New Orleans, had held Mobile locked in a blockade for months. In August of 1864 the old admiral climbed into the rigging of his famous wooden flagship, *Hartford*. At his order the Union fleet fought its way past the Confederate forts guarding the entrance of Mobile Bay.

Immediately the clumsy Confederate ironclad ram, *Tennessee*, steamed for Farragut's ship. One of the admiral's monitors, *The*

Tecumseh, struck a mine—"torpedoes," as they were called. The monitor plunged to the bottom in less than two minutes. The cry went up on the *Hartford*, "Look out ahead! Torpedoes! Torpedoes!"

From the rigging came the admiral's famous answer, "Damn the torpedoes! Full speed ahead!"

The Union fleet steamed into the bay with guns thundering. A rowboat was lowered to pick up men in the water who had escaped from *The Tecumseh* before she plunged to the bottom, and the Confederates did not fire at the men in the rowboat.

The brave sailors in the Confederate ram *Tennessee* tried to take on the entire Federal fleet. Every Union cannon that could be sighted was turned on the ram. The *Hartford* tried to run the ram down and almost foundered herself. The *Hartford* had a narrow escape when she bumped a torpedo, but there was no explosion. Finally, the pounding the ram took began to tell, and the Confederate colors fluttered to the deck. Shortly the forts guarding the harbor surrendered.

It was not a giveaway victory for the North. One hundred and forty-five of Admiral Farragut's sailors lay dead; a hundred and seventy others were wounded.

The news of the victory in Mobile Bay ticked over the wires to the North.

Another Yankee achievement followed: Sherman had captured Atlanta. Although Hood's army had escaped, the fall of Georgia's keystone city meant the end of the southern railway system—a serious thing for the Southern states.

The Northern Democrats now approached McClellan and gave him formal notice that he had been nominated for President. He accepted, but, to his credit and to many people's surprise, he announced he would support the war effort. To do otherwise, he said, would insult the thousands who had died for the Union.

The citizens of the United States went to the polls. They re-elected Abraham Lincoln. This great vote of confidence meant that the people of the North were backing Honest Abe to win the war. This was great news for the soldiers and sailors of the United States. They loved Lincoln and believed in his leadership.

Chapter 27

SHERMAN'S MARCH TO THE SEA

WHEN the Confederate Hood left Atlanta, he attacked the long supply route that was the lifeline of the Union Army, then circled toward Alabama to get more men. He hoped General Sherman would follow.

For a while the Union general was mystified. It was hard to know what Hood was up to. Then Sherman devised an unusual plan. He would not chase General Hood. He would send General Old Pap Thomas and 30,000 men to Nashville to hold the state of Tennessee. As for his own army, Sherman proposed that he march it across Georgia, laying waste to a sixty-mile swath, from Atlanta to Savannah. "I'll make Georgia howl," he said.

When William Tecumseh Sherman telegraphed his plan to Lincoln and Grant, the President was not certain he would approve. He wired General Sherman, "How will you supply your army in enemy territory?"

Sherman replied, "We will live off the country." He would carry a twenty-day supply of emergency rations in his wagon train. For their normal living, his men would take their food from the people of Georgia.

The more President Lincoln thought over General Sherman's

idea, the more he liked it. U. S. Grant was for the plan from the first, for it fell in with what old General Winfield Scott had suggested when the war started: one Federal Army to hold Lee, the Mississippi River to be opened, a Union Army to slash through the South and return to the center and fight Lee.

Lincoln and Grant could see that Sherman's march through one of the richest parts of the South would cause bitterness, but they approved it because it fitted into the best scheme, and because it would show the Confederates their cause was futile and that the Union armies could go where they pleased.

Atlanta was now a forlorn, war-battered city, and it was about to be reduced to ruins. Captain James Crozer wrote his girl back in Iowa from the ravaged town, "... This is the most dilapidated-looking city I have run across in some time. It really made me homesick & was glad to get out of it.... More buildings were burned than intended. Genl Slocum offers $500 reward for the person or persons who set fire to them.... The most prominent buildings are undermined & everything ready to destroy the place. The pride of the South in a few days will be no more...."

The march to the sea started on November 12, 1864. About it Captain Crozer wrote: "I think you may look for us at Savannah, Georgia, sometime in December.... In case the guerrillas molest us or mistreat any of our men, the Corps commanders will mete out the same punishment to citizens.... The order is to destroy all cotton Gin factories & such other buildings as the General sees fit...."

One of the numerous questions that faced General Sherman was what to do with his wounded. He decided to send some to General Thomas in Tennessee; others he would take along in mule-drawn ambulances. Although the wounded were made as comfortable as possible, either trip would be hard on them, particularly for those who would ride in the ambulances on the rough roads across Georgia.

When Sherman was ready, he sent his last message North, cut the telegraph wires, and gave the orders for his army to begin its march.

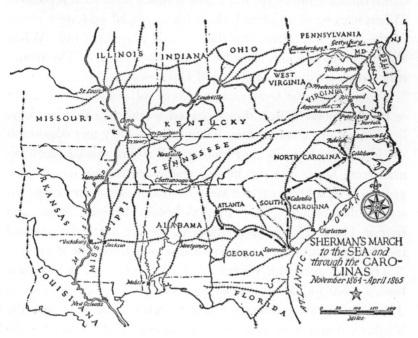

While on the move across Georgia, Captain Crozer wrote:

... Passing through rich country. Plenty of meat of all kinds. Honey, molasses, sweet potatoes. Burnt a lot of cotton and some dwellings. . . . We are fighting the State Militia, old men and young boys. . . . The Sunny South—almost froze last night. Ice was ¾ inch thick. Our blankets wet and froze stiff. Our Cavalry is behaving bad in some cases. . . . We had an interesting time, brought in 50 & 60 head of Horses and Mules. I was put in charge of 12 men and a 2-horse ambulance and told to go out and forage for the regiment. Got a lot of pork, sugar, Chickens, Honey, Molasses, sweet potatoes, Salt, Corn and fodder. . . . They (our men) need watching for today a teamster stole a nigger baby. . . . One of the boys got a violin and had quite a show, one nigger playing & three or four dancing. There is a woman close by our camp who buried her husband alive to save him from us Yanks but it wouldn't answer. They dug him up.

Sherman's army swept on, doing as much damage as it pleased. When it came to a railroad, the soldiers ripped up long sections of the track, built fires with the ties, and heated the rails. When the steel was red hot, they twisted it about a tree. The troops called such a section of rail a "Jeff Davis necktie."

Troops from the western states were still rough frontiersmen at heart. On the march they behaved worse than the men who lived in eastern communities. They killed if they met opposition to their home-burning and looting. All troops missed receiving mail from home and the looting got worse as the march progressed. The soldiers carried away heirlooms, food, anything that struck their fancy. They burned houses, bridges, barns, and fences. The black smoke that rose to the sky every day marked the slow progress of Sherman's 62,000 men across the state.

The Georgians felt pitifully helpless and angry when their homes were looted and robbery committed before their eyes. The Confederate government had no army at hand to stop the Yankees. The whole affair was the bitterest kind of pill for the people of Georgia.

On the march, in Company B of the 73d Illinois, was a sixteen-year-old drummer boy who was an entertainer. His name was William Rodgers and from him sprang a descriptive name for the men on the march. Rodgers spoke of himself as "Bum" Rodgers. At night around the campfire, Rodgers sang an Irish song, each verse of which ended, "Bummers beware! And snoozers take care!" He became known as "Company B's bummer." The word "bummer" spread throughout the army and the men spoke of themselves as "Sherman's bummers." It was a fitting phrase.

Behind the bummers marched an ever-growing mob of Negro

slaves who had run away from their masters to "jine the army." Again a Union Army had the problem of taking care of civilians. The crowd traveled on foot, in wagons, buggies, on mule-back, by oxcart, and in all kinds of costumes. Near Savannah the Southerners increased Sherman's problem by sending 3,000 Negroes out of the city to him with the idea of consuming the Yankees' food, but Sherman's army rolled on.

On December 21 the march to the sea ended. The Union Army had covered 250 miles in forty days. General Sherman entered Savannah and sent President Lincoln a telegram: I BEG TO PRESENT TO YOU AS A CHRISTMAS GIFT, THE CITY OF SAVANNAH, WITH ONE HUNDRED AND FIFTY GUNS, PLENTY OF AMMUNITION, AND ALSO ABOUT 25,000 BALES OF COTTON.

Chapter 28

HOOD ATTACKS IN TENNESSEE

THINGS looked fine for the Union in Savannah when General Sherman sent his telegram to President Lincoln, but in Tennessee a crisis was developing for the United States government. General Hood and 30,000 Confederates were marching north to strike Old Pap Thomas in Nashville.

If General John Hood, the dashing Confederate, could defeat the Rock of Chickamauga, who was commanding Union forces in Tennessee, Hood would be in position to carry the war into Yankee country. In that case, Sherman's march through Georgia would be the worst blunder of the war.

The tall Texan, John Hood, was popular with the Confederates. When his leg was amputated after the Battle of Chickamauga, his soldiers made up a donation of $4,000 so he could buy an artificial limb. They admired his courage and drive. They knew he wanted to *whip Yankees*. John Hood believed in the attack and he was the type men followed in combat.

In his army rode 3,000 horsemen under the great fighter, Nathan Bedford Forrest. With these two leaders showing the way, the Confederates were filled with hope in spite of the fact that many of them were poorly equipped. It takes strong leadership to make barefooted soldiers march and fight.

Sam Dunlop of the First Missouri Battery wrote:

> I was a shoeless Confederate. On the march to Nashville, the Federals made a stand at Columbia on the north side of the Duck River. It was rough country. . . . Two days prior to my arrival at Columbia, my boots entirely deserted my bleeding feet and my barefoot track was plainly visible in the snow. Arriving at a livery barn filled with soldiers trying to dry themselves around some smoky fires, I asked if anyone in there had a pair of shoes to sell or give away. A boy about 15 years standing in the office door said, "Yes. Come in."
>
> He produced a pair of cloth shoes priced at 15 dollars. I gave him a twenty-dollar bill and while he was out hunting change, I spied a pair of heavy leather boots partly covered up by an old Federal overcoat under a bunk in a corner, and when the boy returned they were under *my* coat. . . . Taylor and I left the barn with a step somewhat faster than we had entered. I told Taylor he could have the cloth shoes as they were about two numbers too large for me. The leather shoes were just my fit. . . .

But not all Hood's men were wearing shoes at the Duck River. Here Hood planned to capture the Union troops along the stream.

Old Pap Thomas was back in Nashville, fifty miles away. His commander at the Duck was John Schofield, a capable officer. Schofield's job was to delay Hood, to gain time so Pap could get the army in Nashville ready for a showdown battle.

Schofield's cavalry at the Duck River was under James Wilson, a bald-headed, big-nosed man with a black walrus mustache. General Wilson was a fine cavalryman but he was hard-pressed for horses. To get mounts for his 12,000 men, Wilson had taken horses, with Pap's blessing, from the street railway cars in Nashville, from a circus, and from many farms.

The first brush along the banks of the Duck was between the

cavalry of the two armies. The Yankee cavalry guarded each
ford, and the water in the river was cold and swift. The 2d
Tennessee Confederate Cavalry got over the swollen stream by
making a raft of logs and by fastening them with rope and halter
reins. The twelve volunteers who crossed crept along the bank
and overwhelmed a temporary Union fort that guarded a passage.
Soon all of Forrest's cavalry swam their horses across and the
Federals had to pull back in a hurry to escape capture.

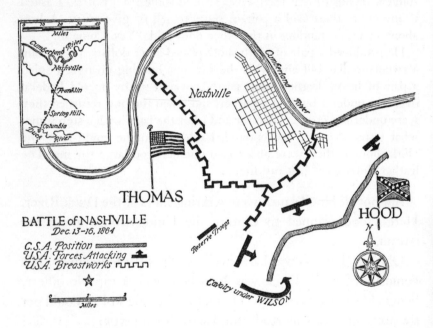

BATTLE of NASHVILLE
Dec. 13-16, 1864

C.S.A. Position
U.S.A. Forces Attacking
U.S.A. Breastworks

At Spring Hill it was the old story again. "*Attack!*" ordered
Hood, although he had little idea what lay ahead. He became
angry at General Benjamin Cheatham, who was away at a dance
when he was needed. Not only did Hood give the brave and
popular General Cheatham the tongue-lashing he deserved, but
Hood led the attack in person. Afterward he wired the Confederate Secretary of War requesting that General Cheatham be

relieved of his command. Then Hood changed his mind several times, finally wiring asking that Cheatham be retained.

Before Hood's army at Franklin, Tennessee, was a strong Union position. The Federals were ready to put up a determined fight, for each day's delay was important to Pap Thomas in Nashville. Pap was working hard to build more trenches at Nashville and to get a makeshift army ready. He was also going over the ground on which he expected to fight, so as to perfect his plan for the main clash.

To save time for General Thomas, Wilson's cavalry slashed at Hood's men near Franklin. General Forrest saw some Confederate soldiers break for the rear. He tried to rally them, without success. A Confederate color-bearer ran past, headed away from the battle. Forrest called for the man to stop, but he did not. Forrest drew his pistol and shot the color-bearer dead, then grabbed the flag and waved it, but he could not stop the panic.

Along the Harpeth River at Franklin some of the hardest fighting of the war took place. Although General Forrest advised General Hood to attack from the flank, Hood ordered thirteen straight-ahead charges against the Yankees, who were using breastworks that had been built earlier in the war. It was slaughter. The Confederates lost many more men than the Yankees, including six of their generals.

When General Schofield and his men dragged wearily in from the battle at Franklin, Old Pap Thomas greeted them with hot coffee and food before he put them in position so he could use them against Hood.

Hood came on. In reality, his army had been compressing a spring ever since it attacked on the Duck River, twenty-one days before. That spring was getting harder and harder to push back, and the Confederate Army was becoming weaker. Hood had almost dashed his army to pieces at Franklin. The men in gray were in no shape to attack, nor could they retreat with Old Pap Thomas lying behind the entrenchments at Nashville waiting to see what they would do.

Back east General Grant was worried. He did not know the situation in Nashville accurately, and he thought that General Thomas was delaying his attack too long. Old Pap had never been one of his favorite generals. U. S. Grant bombarded Pap with telegrams urging him to attack. The Union could not afford to have Hood pull a trick and escape to raid the North.

General Thomas was calm. He wired Washington he would attack when he thought conditions were right. The weather had changed and ice lay over the landscape, which made it difficult to move cavalry and artillery, for the horses slipped. General Halleck wired back to Pap, "Lieutenant General Grant is dissatisfied with your delay in attacking the enemy." But Pap was undisturbed. He telegraphed he would attack as soon as he could.

Grant lost patience. He selected General John Logan to take Pap's place and ordered Logan to head for Tennessee, take command, and attack Hood. It looked to the Union leaders as if the Rock of Chickamauga had lost his desire to fight. Grant worried some more, then he got on a train and headed for Nashville to see for himself.

The weather thawed and Pap Thomas attacked.

His cavalry, under General Wilson, swept around the Confederate left. They were unopposed, for Hood had his cavalryman, Forrest, off on a mission. Pap's infantry was massed at a key point and it smashed the Confederate line. Hood's army found itself in a gigantic nutcracker.

When General Logan got news of the success of Pap's attack, he stopped. There was no need for any general to replace Thomas. General Grant stopped also, for the reports indicated that Old Pap Thomas had fought one of the best-planned battles of the war. U. S. Grant sent Pap a wire of congratulations and returned to the siege of Petersburg.

Hood's Army of the Tennessee was ruined. The remnants of his army fought a brave retreat toward Alabama but so many of them were lost in the fight against Thomas they were never again a threat to the North.

Chapter 29

SHERMAN IN THE CAROLINAS

Aᖴᴛᴇʀ resting his men in Savannah for almost a month, General Sherman got ready to strike again. His army had enjoyed its stay in Savannah; the men had eaten their fill of oysters and had made acquaintances in the town. Sherman held a grand review to make sure that his army of more than sixty thousand men was ready to march to Virginia.

The army was ready to move north, but it was undisciplined, even by Civil War standards. Captain James Crozer wrote:

... We left on Jan. 14, 1865, and marched to the dock & loaded on board the steamer *Crescent* that would take us thirty-five miles up the coast to Beaufort, S. C. The *Crescent* was already loaded with wagons, Ambulances, Horses & Mules. The boys were put on upper deck & crowded pretty close. The officers had the cabin which was comfortable. The ocean was just rough enough to make the men feel little sick. ... Arrived at Beaufort. When our soldiers found we would not land at the dock untill morning, they crowded into the officers' cabin to have a good place to sleep. Maj. Lubbers not liking the performance, detailed a guard at the door to keep all out except commissioned officers. That made the boys mad. To have revenge they all went up on deck & commenced dancing & throwing bullets through skylights. At last I put a stop to it. ...

The red-bearded General Sherman knew that his army faced a harder march than the picnic across Georgia. Confederate leaders were figuring some way to try to stop Sherman. "Little Joe" Johnston was placed in command of scanty Confederate forces which would be outnumbered by the Federals. The country would also be a hindrance. The Union general wanted to go to Columbia, South Carolina, then to Fayetteville, and Goldsboro, North Carolina. Part of the way his men would have to travel through dreary swamps. Infantry could travel all right through the swamps, but it would take real work to get the artillery guns and caissons through. Again there would be no supply lines. This meant no government rations for Sherman's men, no extra ammunition, no newspapers, no letters from home. The worries of the people of the Carolinas were *much* greater.

On the march, Crozer wrote:

... Any amount of Contrabands [1] coming in. I don't see what's to become of them. We are hard at work corduroying the roads in the swamps and have used many a mile of rail fence to make the muddy roads passable. ... Before leaving today, made a bonfire of a house to warm oneself by. ... Two or three pretty fair plantations. The boys made bonfires of the houses. ... Now no houses to be burned except by order of Div. Commanders but the boys pay little attention to the order.

Joe Johnston's Confederate soldiers had little effect on Sherman's bummers, who did almost as they pleased. Crozer described it in a letter:

... Stopped at one house very nicely furnished. Several young ladies around. They were rebels but claimed protection. ... We ran

[1] Contrabands—name applied to Negroes by the Union general, Benjamin F. Butler. He called fugitive slaves who came into Northern lines "contrabands," meaning they could be employed to help the Union cause. The Southerners used the word, too, applying it to slaves impressed to work on their fortifications. The Negroes themselves liked it and would often say when they appeared in Union lines, "We's contraband."

on to three horses & two mules tied in the swamps & two wagons loaded with Meat & Corn. Also found nice open buggy. We harnessed up one of the mules, loaded the buggy with the best meat & started for camp. I led two horses & a mule. . . .

The foraging and pillaging went on. Sherman's army was determined to make South Carolina "the worst riddled state in the Confederacy."

". . . It is hard to see the sufferings among the citizens where the army has passed through," wrote Captain Crozer. "Everything in the line of provisions taken, houses ransacked if not burned. . . . Had to wade through mud & water waist deep. Our battery opened fire & that scattered the Johnnies in all directions."

Just ahead lay Columbia, South Carolina. Confederate cavalry held the town. Sherman's army shelled it, routed the Southern cavalry, and marched in. The citizens made the mistake of treating the Union soldiers to whiskey in an effort to get their good will. Chaos resulted.

In Captain Crozer's letters appears this account:

Columbia is a very nice place, wide streets and shade trees, some very fine residences and splendid yards. The State House has cost over a million dollars. . . . The Rebs before leaving set fire to some cotton piled in the streets. Strong winds blowing caught some of the houses. The 3d Brigade, nearly all tight, and instead of trying to save the houses, helped the fire along. . . . It was the most thrilling sight I ever witnessed over three quarters of the town is in ashes. . . . The liquor made the boys worse than demons.

Later, General Sherman also stated that, in his opinion, the Southern cavalry set fire to the cotton, but Confederate authorities claimed the cotton was set afire by Federal troops. There is no doubt that strong winds moved the fire to the buildings and, as a result, the town burned.

When the march proceeded, Captain Crozer wrote:

... We are living pretty much off the country, foraging. Issued us two days' rations the last seven days. ... I don't see how the people of this State are going to live. ... The Rebels shot eleven foragers and put them in a pile with a headboard reading, "Fate of all foragers."

Behind the army was an ever-growing column of "contrabands." One of Sherman's major generals, Henry Slocum, wrote:

... The spectacle was both comical and pitiful. ... These poor creatures brought all their earthly goods, horses, mules, cows, dogs, carts, old stagecoaches, family carriages, and lumber wagons filled with bedding, cooking utensils, and "traps" of all kinds. ... The firing of a musket or pistol brought a panic to these people.

It was necessary to feed the "contrabands" as well as the troops on the march. With so many Negroes going north, many wondered what the South would do for laborers.

When the army marched into the pine forests of North Carolina, it set fire to the woods. This meant that many soldiers and the long columns of Negroes had to march through smoke and sparks.

Despite an order from General Slocum, the foraging went on. Crozer wrote his girl:

... Cotton & paper mills burnt. There was between three & four hundred women employed in the cotton factory and it turned out from three to five thousand yards of cotton cloth per day. ... There was nothing left in the country for the women to eat. Some of them came along with us.

At Bentonville, near Goldsboro, the Confederate Army offered serious resistance but was defeated by Sherman's veterans. More Union soldiers joined his army, swelling it to nearly 90,000.

Fortunately, his army no longer lived off the countryside, for rations were shipped to it from the North.

The mission of striking through the South had been accomplished, but long-lasting bitterness had been created, especially where Sherman's men had ravaged and pillaged.

Chapter 30

THE END OF THE WAR

DURING the nine-month siege at Petersburg both sides dug a network of trenches. Lee proved that he was one of the great generals of all time. With only 57,000 soldiers he was able to fend off General Grant's huge army of 124,700.

Lee's force was in bad shape because the food supply was a problem not even he could solve. Almost every night a handful of his men deserted, yet the thousands who remained were determined to fight on as long as "Marse Robert" was at their head. The fact that his men had the will to fight against great odds when they were on the verge of starvation gives an insight into the leadership of Robert E. Lee.

To try to upset General Grant and to gain a crushing victory, General Lee planned an attack against a Union stronghold east of the besieged city. The place was known as Fort Stedman. To lead the attack, he selected one of his best officers, a man who had seen much fighting, General John Gordon.

At three in the morning Gordon and his men crept quietly from the Confederate lines to the fort. The Union sentries awoke Grant's men just in time and vicious hand-to-hand fighting occurred. Gordon's Confederates seized the fort but they were confused by the vast network of trenches. The Union position did not look as they had visualized it. Many Southern units became separated in the fight. Finally, Gordon's men were driven back while the cannons raked them. No one has accurately determined how many Confederates were lost in this before-dawn attack.

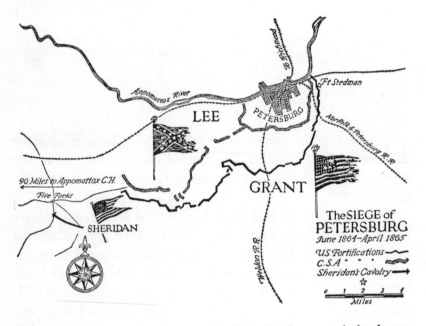

The failure of the plan to take Fort Stedman and the heavy losses were a shock to Lee. Hoping to make a recovery, he took 15,000 men out of the trenches and all of his cavalry and sent them on a wide sweep to Five Forks. He hoped to surprise Grant with a blow from the left.

At Five Forks the dashing Phil Sheridan with his Union cavalry ("critter boys," the Union infantrymen called them) clashed with the desperate Confederates. In the heat of battle, the energetic Sheridan was at his best. To rally his hard-pressed troops, he seized his crimson-and-white battle flag and spurred his tremendous horse into the fight. Sheridan waved the banner over his head to encourage his men.

During the battle, Sheridan called on Brigadier General Ranald Mackenzie, three years out of West Point. Sheridan ordered young Mackenzie to take a cavalry division around behind the Confederates and attack them from the rear. The Confederates were surprised and, after 2,500 had been killed, 4,000 others held up their hands.

Back in Richmond, a lawless Southern element threatened to control the city. Living was already difficult. It took sixty dollars of Confederate money to buy a breakfast, and from five hundred to seven hundred to buy a pair of boots. Butter sold for fifteen dollars a pound.

When the news of the Federal victories at Petersburg and Five Forks reached Richmond, President Davis and his civilian officials left the city. The Confederates set fire to warehouses and arsenals about the town. A mob took over and looting began.

Seventy miles from Richmond General Lee was still trying to overwhelm a larger force. At Appomattox Court House, Sheridan's cavalry clashed with Lee's leading regiments. General Lee ordered an attack and the cavalry was driven back, but large forces of Federal infantry appeared. The Confederates were surrounded. There was nothing for General Lee to do but surrender. Further bloodshed would gain nothing, so he sent a white linen dishcloth to General Grant as a sign of truce. The date was April 9, 1865.

The two great generals met in a brick house at Appomattox for General Lee's surrender. Lee wore his best gray uniform. About his waist was a yellow silk sash. He had a gold sword and clean gauntlets. His horse, Traveller, was carefully groomed. General Grant, in a muddy uniform, part of which was a private's blouse, apologized to Lee for his unkempt appearance.

At this moment, not far from the brick house, a flashy young general, George Custer, galloped up to the Confederate fighter, General Old Pete Longstreet, and demanded his surrender. Longstreet knew of Custer's vanity and love of the limelight. The old Confederate flared, "General Lee is talking to General Grant. We will not recognize a subordinate. Now go! Or I will teach you a lesson you will not forget. *Go!*" Custer spurred his horse away, leaving the surrender details to his superiors, Grant and Lee.

Inside the brick house General Lee cleaned his steel-rimmed spectacles and listened to General Grant chat about old army times and Mexican War days. Finally, the Confederate leader reminded General Grant that he was present to surrender his army. Quietly, Lee asked for terms.

Sam Grant's terms were fair. He allowed the Confederates to

keep their horses because he knew they would be needing them for the spring plowing and because food was scarce in every part of the South. Grant also realized that Lee's army was starving. The Union leader turned to Little Phil Sheridan and asked, "How many rations do you have?" When Sheridan had replied, Grant said, "Give General Lee food for 25,000 men." Grant was taking the first steps toward bringing the country back together.

All Confederate materials of war except side arms were surrendered, and the Confederates were paroled. General Lee thanked General Grant for his generous terms.

Now came General Lee's hardest job. He had to face his men. When he rode Traveller away from the house toward his army, General Grant raised his hat in salute. Lee's Army of Northern Virginia gathered about their leader. "Are we surrendered?" they called. Lee had to tell them. There was a heartrending silence. The Confederate soldiers pressed close to Traveller. They wanted to touch General Lee's clothing or his horse. Down the line a band on horses from the 1st New York (Lincoln) Cavalry played "Home Sweet Home." Strong men wept.

When the Union troops entered partially ruined Richmond, President Lincoln paid that city a visit. He looked at the house President Jefferson Davis had occupied, and he visited Libby Prison, which only recently had held hundreds of Union soldiers as prisoners of war. The Union general, Godfrey Weitzel, asked President Lincoln how the conquered Southern people should be treated. Lincoln replied that he did not desire to issue orders on that subject, but he said, "If I were in your place I'd let 'em up easy, let 'em up easy."

In Charleston Harbor, five days later, five thousand Federal soldiers, sailors, and Northern civilians held a ceremony at Fort Sumter. Robert Anderson raised the same flag that he had

hauled down at the fort's surrender four years before. In a brief
speech General Anderson thanked God that he had lived to
see the flag of the United States fly again over the fort, and he
prayed for peace. The multitude responded, "Amen! Amen!"
Bands played, and the crowd sang "The Star-Spangled Banner."
A salute to the flag was fired from every United States Army
cannon around the harbor as well as from every naval vessel.

That night tragedy struck at Ford's Theater in Washington. A
crazed assassin, John Wilkes Booth, entered the presidential box,
shot Abraham Lincoln in the back of the head, and leaped to the
stage, all before the audience realized what had happened. Booth
ran from the building and escaped on his horse. The next morning the President died.

Abraham Lincoln's death was a shock to the nation. The people in the South as well as in the North were crushed. The
Southerners felt that the great President could have welded the
country back together. They were not sure of the ability of the
Vice-President, Andrew Johnson, for he did not have Lincoln's
feeling for people, nor his reputation for fair play. The Confederate prisoners, still locked in Federal prisons, were in danger
from cruel guards and others who thought that Lincoln's assas-
sination was a Southern plot. Gloom spread over the Union
Army. The Negroes were confused. Many of them believed that
Lincoln had *personally* freed them. They were afraid, uncertain
what lay ahead for them.

Handbills appeared in the streets:

$100,000 REWARD!

THE MURDERER

of our late-beloved President, Abraham Lincoln

IS STILL AT LARGE

After a hysterical two-week search by the army and the secret service, John Wilkes Booth was trapped in a barn in Virginia. The barn was set afire. Booth was shot either by himself or by his pursuers, who sprayed bullets into the building.

News of other surrenders tempered the grief of the people in the North. General Joe Johnston received generous terms from General Sherman. Confederate forces in Louisiana and Texas surrendered.

In the Deep South Jefferson Davis was trying to get to Mississippi, where he hoped to rally Southern sympathizers and continue the war. He was captured by Union cavalry in Georgia. With him was much of the gold in the Confederate treasury. Many Southerners resented Davis' action. They felt he should have surrendered in a dignified manner, as Lee had done, instead of trying to escape. Davis was taken to Fortress Monroe, Virginia, where he was imprisoned for two years. At the end of that time Union authorities wisely let him go. They did not wish to see Jefferson Davis become a martyr in the eyes of the Southern people.

The regiments of General Sherman's army raced each other on the way north to see who could arrive first in Washington for their final review. The regiments would have reveille at three or four in the morning and march rapidly out of camp, often only to wait at a crossroad while some other unit passed.

The Grand Review of the Union Army in Washington, which took place in late May before the soldiers were allowed to go home, was a magnificent spectacle. Many of the soldiers had been up all night before the parade polishing sabers and equipment. The Army of the Potomac marched the first day. General Meade, the winning general at the Battle of Gettysburg, was the first to ride by the presidential reviewing stand at the White House. Close behind the general rode a sergeant from the 1st

Massachusetts Cavalry carrying the headquarters flag of the army. Cheering crowds lined Pennsylvania Avenue. The bands played "Hail to the Chief" and other stirring marches as the troops swung along. Across the face of the Capitol hung a large sign reading, "THE ONLY NATIONAL DEBT WE CAN NEVER PAY IS THE DEBT WE OWE TO THE VICTORIOUS UNION SOLDIERS."

On the second day William Sherman's army passed in review. Captain Crozer, in one of his last letters home, wrote:

> ... At the signal gun we started down the avenue. Streets, houses, housetops & every available point was crowded. Singing cheering clapping of hands & waving of flags greeted us on all sides. Bouquets & wreaths were plenty. I got a very nice one and placed it on our colors. The boys done splendidly never saw them do better. Everybody praised us & said we done better and looked finer than the Potomac Army....

In Nashville, Old Pap Thomas published an order praising the men who had fought for him. He was the senior officer present and he ordered a review of his army. As his men passed before him for the last time, many realized that they were looking at the strong and kindly face of one of the greatest Union generals.

The great Civil War was over. There was no shouting or band to play stirring airs when hundreds of thousands of wounded and crippled soldiers limped home. Nor was there glory for the thousands of wrecked men in prison camps. The people of the North had a problem caring for these men. The South faced even greater problems.

The greatest tragedy of the war was not the destruction of untold billions of dollars' worth of property, nor the expenditure of other billions to wage war, nor the hate developed in combat and nursed in prison camps, nor the bitterness created by forays of invading troops. The great tragedy was the lives that were lost. Nothing can replace the blood of brave men. Today, a hundred years after the cannons pounded Fort Sumter, the wounds of the war are healing, but our nation still feels the loss of more than half a million Americans. No one knows what these virile men or their descendants might have achieved for our country.

FOR FURTHER READING

FOR FURTHER READING

In writing *The Story of the Civil War*, I referred to many volumes. My principal guideposts were:

Summaries of Selected Military Campaigns, Department of Military Art and Engineering, United States Military Academy, West Point, New York, 1953 and 1941. *American Military History, 1607–1953*, Department of the Army, 1956. *Battles and Leaders of the Civil War*, The Century Company, New York, 1888. *Ordeal by Fire*, by Fletcher Pratt, William Sloane Associates, New York, 1948. *The Story of the Confederacy*, by Robert Self Henry, Bobbs-Merrill, Indianapolis, 1931, 1936. *Robert E. Lee*, by Earl Schenck Miers, Alfred A. Knopf, New York, 1956. *Army Letters, 1861–1865*, by Oliver Wilcox Norton, O. L. Deming, Chicago, 1903. Numerous unit histories were consulted to advantage.

SELECTED BOOKS

ASHLEY, ROBERT P. *The Stolen Train*. Philadelphia and Toronto: John C. Winston Company, 1953.

AVIRETT, REVEREND, JAMES B. *The Memoirs of General Turner Ashby and His Compeers*. Baltimore: 1867.

BAKER, NINA BROWN. *Cyclone in Calico*. Boston: Little, Brown & Co., 1952.

BIRCHER, WILLIAM. *A Drummer-Boy's Diary*. St. Paul, Minnesota: 1889.

CATTON, BRUCE. "Lincoln's Difficult Decisions," *Civil War History Magazine*. Iowa City: June, 1956.

———. *U. S. Grant and the American Military Tradition*. Boston: Little, Brown & Co., 1954.

CLEAVES, FREEMAN. *Rock of Chickamauga*. Norman, Oklahoma: University of Oklahoma Press, 1948.

COCKE, PRESTON. *The Battle of New Market*. Richmond, Virginia: 1914.

Confederate Military History. Atlanta, Georgia: 1899.

Confederate Veteran, Vols. V, VII, XIII, and XXXIII.

DOUGLAS, HENRY KYD. *I Rode with Stonewall*. Chapel Hill, North Carolina: University of North Carolina Press, 1940.

DOWDEY, CLIFFORD. *The Land They Fought For*. New York: Doubleday & Co., Inc., 1955.

FREEMAN, DOUGLAS SOUTHALL. *Lee's Lieutenants*. New York: Charles Scribner's Sons, 1946.

FREMANTLE, SIR ARTHUR JAMES LYON. *The Fremantle Diary*. Edited by Walter Lord. Boston: Little, Brown & Co., 1954.

GRANT, U. S. *Personal Memoirs of U. S. Grant*. New York: 1885.

HERR, MAJOR GENERAL JOHN K., and WALLACE, EDWARD S. *The Story of the U. S. Cavalry*. Boston: Little Brown & Co., 1953.

HILL, EDWIN C. *Fort Sumter Memorial*. New York: 1915.

HULL, SUSAN R. *Boy Soldiers of the Confederacy*. New York and Washington: Neale Pub. Co., 1905.

JACKSON, MARY ANNA, MRS. *Memoirs of Stonewall Jackson*. Louisville, Kentucky: 1895.

JACOBS, BRUCE. *Heroes of the Army*. New York: W. W. Norton & Company, Inc., 1956.

KEILEY, ANTHONY M. *In Vinculis, or The Prisoner of War*. Petersburg, Virginia: 1866.

KIEFFER, REVEREND HENRY MARTYN. *The Recollections of a Drummer Boy*. Boston: Houghton Mifflin Company, 1883.

LAWTON, EBA ANDERSON. *Major Robert Anderson and Fort Sumter*. 1861.

LYKES, RICHARD W. *Billy Mahone of Virginia*. Petersburg, Virginia: 1953.

LYTLE, ANDREW NELSON. *Bedford Forrest and His Critter Company*. New York: G. P. Putnam's Sons, 1931.

MACARTNEY, CLARENCE EDWARD NOBLE. *Lincoln and His Generals*. Philadelphia: Dorrance & Company, Inc., 1925.

MITCHELL, JOSEPH B., LIEUTENANT COLONEL. *Decisive Battles of the Civil War*. New York: G. P. Putnam's Sons, 1955.

OWEN, MARIE BANKHEAD. *The Story of Alabama*. New York: Lewis Historical Publishing Company, 1949.

THOMAS, CLARENCE. *General Turner Ashby, The Centaur of the South*. Winchester, Virginia: 1907.

WILLIAMS, T. HARRY. *Lincoln and His Generals*. New York: Alfred A. Knopf, Inc., 1952.

WILLIAMS, T. HARRY. *P. G. T. Beauregard—Napoleon in Gray*. Baton Rouge: Louisiana State University Press, 1955.

WILLIAMSON, JAMES J. *Mosby's Rangers*. New York: Sturgis & Walton, 1909.

INDEX

INDEX